Shine

Shine

Making the most of life without losing yourself

SAMANTHA ARMYTAGE

hachette
AUSTRALIA

IMPORTANT NOTE TO READERS: Although every effort has been made to
ensure that the contents of this book are accurate, it must not be treated as a substitute
for qualified medical advice. Always consult a qualified medical practitioner. Neither
the author nor the publisher can be held responsible for any loss or claim arising out
of the use, or misuse, of the suggestions made or the failure to take professional medical advice.

 hachette
AUSTRALIA

Published in Australia and New Zealand in 2014
by Hachette Australia
(an imprint of Hachette Australia Pty Limited)
Level 17, 207 Kent Street, Sydney NSW 2000
www.hachette.com.au

10 9 8 7 6 5 4 3 2 1

National Library of Australia
Cataloguing-in-Publication data:

Armytage, Samantha, author.
Shine: making the most of life without losing yourself/Samantha Armytage.

978 0 7336 3344 7 (paperback)

Life skills.
Social learning.
Conduct of life.
Self-actualization (Psychology).

302.2

Cover design by Christabella Designs
Cover photograph courtesy of Tarsha Hosking/Seven Network
Text design by Kinart
Typeset in Minion Pro Regular by Kirby Jones
Printed and bound in Australia by Griffin Press, Adelaide, an accredited ISO AS/NZS 14001:2009
Environmental Management System printer

FSC
www.fsc.org
MIX
Paper from
responsible sources
FSC® C009448

The paper this book is printed on is certified against the Forest Stewardship
Council® Standards. Griffin Press holds FSC chain of custody certification
SGS-COC-005088. FSC promotes environmentally responsible, socially beneficial
and economically viable management of the world's forests.

For my darling niece, Lucia,

may you love all the days of your life.

I hope you manage to avoid all Auntie Sammy's mistakes ...

but if you can't avoid them – I hope you have as much fun as I have

trying to work them all out! xx

Contents

Introduction

$\mathcal{H}$i there,

Thanks for picking up my book. *Shine* is the story of a girl from the bush who dreamed of being a vet but instead fell into journalism. She used to wear her retainer at university (six years after she got her braces off!), thought she'd be married by twenty-eight and still can't do her own hair.

I have never considered myself to be terribly glamorous, sophisticated or in any position to give anyone else advice, but lately, with so much going on in my life, I realised this is not my first rodeo.

I have made it to a fairly decent age on my lonesome, found success in my life and had a whole lot of fun along the way. I have learned a lot, laughed A LOT, cried A LOT and lived a lot.

I've survived boarding school, dated some appalling men (and some lovely ones), travelled the world, made some lasting and true friendships with women, dieted a bit, weathered some mean girls, learned to navigate office politics, bought and sold property, cars and livestock entirely ON MY OWN and carved out a ripper of a career in television.

Along the way, I've developed a love and appreciation of health and well-being, and tried to balance that with my love of a party.

I've grown up to embrace my body and I now relish being strong – both physically and mentally.

I've learned to set goals, eat right, move more, organise my life, live with flair, be a woman of substance, appreciate my family, rise above things, open my mind and be the leading lady in the movie of my life. If only I could talk to my younger self and let her know it was going to be okay. This is why I want to share what I've learned and am still learning – I can be like that sister/aunt/ friend, the one who helps out and talks about their own ups and downs.

I want you to be the best person you can be, because that's good for the sisterhood. Behind every great woman are some terrific girlfriends, a wicked investment portfolio, the recipe for a mean mojito and shapewear.

So, I'd like you to consider me something of a 'big sister' – bossing you around like I did to my siblings Georgie and Charlie.

I hope *Shine* can guide you through life a little.

If nothing else, learn from my mistakes.

Mostly I just hope *Shine* makes you feel like you're not alone.

Us girls need to stick together.

We're ALL fallible, we ALL make mistakes and we ALL have the same moments of neediness and loneliness.

None of us really knows what we're doing on this planet – we're all just doing our best in the world. (A phrase I often use!)

We need to stop competing with one another and start supporting each other in our choices and help each other when we stuff up.

I'm hoping this book will start you thinking, planning and realising your gifts. My most important message is to learn to love yourself and love your life, because you only get one (unless you're a Hindu) and it's TOO DAMN SHORT.

Enjoy the read,

Sam x

Setting goals

CHAPTER ONE

*I*n late 2001, after three years working as a lowly paid TV reporter
in Canberra, I decided something had to change. My dream was to
work as a news reporter at a metro station in Sydney or Melbourne.
I mailed off CVs to every network and knocked on the doors of every
news director. Nothing. Nada. Zip.

I thought I was a reasonable reporter and had further to go in the
industry, but I did question whether or not TV was for me. I thought I
might give print journalism a go. A family friend had recently married
a great girl, who happened to be the daughter of the boss of the
publishing house Condé Nast in New York. As this was before email
(I may not be young), I rang my friend and asked if he would mind
passing on the name of a young, keen Aussie addicted to *Sex and the
City* who was willing to work on any magazine (even making coffee!).
It was hastily and very kindly arranged that I would go to New York,

maybe start on Architectural Digest *and (in my mind, anyway) work my way up to* Vogue.

The day before I planned to hand in my resignation, my phone rang. It was Sky News offering me the role of political correspondent in the Canberra Press Gallery. It was a Sliding Doors *moment. Should I run off to join Carrie and the girls in the Big Apple? Or stay in Canberra? Perhaps astonishingly, I chose Canberra.*

I felt I was on the right path, but there was a lot of hard work ahead so I should get serious about my career, and start setting some goals. As a teenager and through university into my twenties, I was not a goal-setter. In fact I went the other way and deliberately didn't plan anything. I was having a lot of fun and anything I did try to plan always ended up not panning out and heading in another – usually much better – direction. So I'd always thought, why bother planning?

It was only when I reached my thirties that I actually took goal-setting really seriously. I guess that's what happens as you start to mature; for me, real maturity didn't start until my thirties. I blame boarding school!

Being in your thirties can be such a wonderful time for a woman. It is for me. It's when, I believe, you come into your own. You connect to your inner strength and really start to feel your power. This stirs in your twenties, roars during your thirties and, I hope, skyrockets in your forties!

To start this process of connection to yourself and setting some goals, the first step is to identify your values.

What makes you tick?

Take some time to sit quietly, perhaps in a yoga class, or when you're stuck in traffic, or on the bus home, and reflect on who and what you are. Ask yourself what you believe in. When you get home, write your thoughts down. This will give you an internal reference point and influence your behaviour – it will act as a sort of backbone, if you like.

These will be values your parents instilled in you, or lessons you've learned through your life – often by making the wrong decisions and working out what you don't want, and the things you won't stand for any longer. Perhaps they're traits you like in other people and want to emulate.

If you want to change for the better, you can start by 'faking it till you make it'. Create a 'brand' that represents your core beliefs in your mind.

It might sound crazy, but it will help you remember and protect your values. In a notebook, I have written down the words I would like attached to my name when people talk about me behind my back. Scrawled all over the page are the following:

- Honesty
- Achievement
- Brave
- Bold
- Calm
- Determined
- Original
- Generous
- Health-orientated
- Family
- Country
- Financial independence
- Practical
- Capable
- Resilient
- Approval (seeking)
- Playful
- Intuition
- Humour
- Curious
- Creative
- Perfectionist

… to name just a few. (There are plenty more, but I don't want this book to be all about me. Haha!)

These words remind me who I am when the going gets a bit tough and I forget to hold my own hand through life. One look at this page shows me where I came from, and where I want to go. Try to keep these values positive and keep them private if you like, but have them in the back of your mind.

Being true to your values

You'll be surprised how empowering it is to be true to yourself in your everyday life. Some aspects of your belief system will become more or less relevant as you go through different stages of your life, but your core values should remain the same.

For example, I was *raised* to be honest, respectful and hardworking. I *choose* to have fun in my life and not take myself too seriously. I have spent many years working on my patience and tolerance, listening to my gut instinct and really backing myself.

In my early days reporting news in Sydney I was sent to do what's called a 'death knock'. These are awful assignments when someone has died and you are sent to interview the family. This particular story was so awful (there were children involved) that I could not bring myself to knock on the door. The cameraman and I sat in the car then rang the office and said there was no one home.

I know I didn't do my job properly that day, but I think I'm a better person for it.

WHAT DO YOU WANT TO BE WHEN YOU GROW UP?

Never stop asking yourself this question. Some of the most together, seemingly successful professionals still don't know. They keep doing what they're doing because they don't know what else to do.

I actually still don't feel grown up and keep dreaming of my ideal job. Even though the one I have is pretty awesome – it pays to have some back-up plans when you work in TV!

Life's too short to only do one thing. I would *love* to write for *The Simpsons*, or write a sitcom, or work in some kind of interiors styling. I'm not ready to do any of these things just yet but it's nice to have them to dream about. I know I also want to live by a lake, and have a veggie garden. They will have to wait too, but I know one day they will come.

Be ambitious

When you're setting goals for yourself, don't hold back, be ambitious. My name is often prefixed with the word 'ambitious' in newspaper and magazine articles in a negative sense. The really baffling thing is I've found these articles are mostly written by women. I find this really hurtful as I've never once seen a young(ish) male journalist being described as ambitious. Believe me, they all are.

What's wrong with a woman being ambitious? In her inspirational book *Lean In*, Facebook Chief Operating Officer Sheryl Sandberg talks a lot about female ambition and does so brilliantly. 'Aggressive and hard-charging women violate unwritten rules about acceptable social conduct. Men are continually applauded for being ambitious and powerful and successful, but women who display these same traits often pay a social penalty. Female accomplishments come at a cost.'

Let's get this clear, it's okay for women to be ambitious. It's taken me a long time to acknowledge my ambitious side. When people asked me as a little girl what I wanted to be when I grew up, I'd blush and say 'a mother'. Being a mother is, of course, a lovely and fulfilling life choice – my mother and many of the women in my family didn't work outside the home.

When people these days describe me as a 'career girl' I still feel a little stab of annoyance. I simply declare that I am putting a roof over my own head because someone has to. I've had a good run – I fell into a career I am passionate about, and once I realised that, I worked like crazy.

I never thought of myself as hugely ambitious, but I must have been to get to where I am now. I think about some of the work situations where it appears my spine has been made into steel, and I actually feel proud.

I've had to toughen up and I don't apologise for that. I've looked around the newsroom at other, older women, and watched closely. I've seen some female journalists adopt male behaviours such as aggression, which I don't think is necessary but I understand why it happens and I've tried really hard to celebrate my femininity. I believe I've achieved this, while still standing up for my beliefs and reaching my career goals.

Remember this saying: the higher a monkey climbs, the more you can see of its bottom. With ambition comes success. With success comes privilege and with privilege comes responsibility. Arm yourself with this knowledge, and embrace the challenge of achieving what you want from your career.

Find your passion

Try to find your passion. Ask yourself:

- What makes me happy?
- Where am I happy?
- Who am I happy with?

Decide whether you are going to be passive and let life happen to you, or whether you are going to get out there, follow your passions and be a creator. My yoga instructor, Kate, worked in finance and tolerated it. Loving her yoga classes on the weekends, she took a huge risk, leaving her job and retraining in something she really enjoyed doing. Now she has me, half of Sydney and the South Sydney Rabbitohs NRL team queueing to be taught by her. She also teaches the yoga teachers, writes books and hosts retreats.

Most importantly, she is one of the most divine, content, calm and focused women I know. She was also younger than me at boarding school. Another quick life lesson: always remember that how you behave towards someone may one day come back to haunt you. One day Kate told me I was the Year Twelve girl sitting on her dining-room table when she started boarding in Year Seven. I couldn't remember but the dining room was terrifying when you were twelve and you'd just been sent away to school. When I asked her if I was nice to her, she said I was. Phew.

I ask myself what it is about television I like and how I would be without it. Sometimes being in the public eye is awful and I complain about it, but if it was all taken away from me how would I feel about that?

I enjoy telling a story and informing people. I like sharing with people and I like helping people. But I would like to be a better interviewer and I would love to have more balance in my life. I know I still have lots to learn – and that's exciting. It keeps life interesting.

For example, ask yourself:

- What is it about my friendships that I like?
- What is it about staying healthy that I like?

I love my friends to be loyal and honest but I need to spend more time with them and listen to them more. I need to work on being more spontaneous, maybe texting them when I think about them instead of disappearing for months on end. (They're a very understanding mob, my mates!) I need to be healthy, strong and vital to do my job. I would like to be more flexible at yoga – my goal is to do a flat-footed downward dog, almost there! And I would also like to look better in jeans. There you have it.

Take stock

Sit yourself down and give yourself a good talking to. Are you racing through life, doing a job that doesn't make you happy, going to a gym you loathe because you think you need to, and hanging out with emotional vampires? If you can afford it, I recommend taking yourself off somewhere quiet, like a health retreat. Yoga retreats are also fabulous weekends away, usually full of like-minded, busy, supportive people.

A 'digital detox', where you give up any kind of digital device for a set period of time, will also help you focus, which can be very hard to do in our day-to-day lives. Sit quietly with yourself, which can sometimes be scary. Reflection is really hard work, which is probably why we don't do it very often. Let your mind go still and explore where you're at – and where you want to be. If you're not happy inside, it's going to affect everyone around you. Believe me, I've been there.

Clear your mind

In order to take stock, know your values, find your passion and set some life goals. You need to throw out everything that's broken. That includes:

- Jobs you hate
- Friends who are bad for you
- Boyfriends who make you feel bad about yourself
- Clothes you haven't worn for two years
- Cups with the handles missing
- Bank accounts you no longer use
- Gym equipment at home you haven't sat on/walked on/rowed on for two years
- Old shabby bed linen and tea towels.

Cull the contents of your house. Clean your car. Declutter your desk. Know where everything in your life is. You never know when you may need to grab it in a hurry. If your mind is free of clutter you can think clearly about where your life is going.

Acknowledge your successes

How do you measure success? As women, we really need to stop being so hard on ourselves. It's important to recognise when we've done well. It's not conceited, it's what we work hard for.

After I was handed the *Sunrise* co-hosting job, I bought myself a silver bangle from Tiffany's that I had been eyeing off for ages. It was expensive and beautiful and I love it. And it was a well-deserved treat to myself for all my hard work as a journo over the years (which still continues!).

You do need to recognise reaching your goals on a deeper level. The best reward you can ever give yourself is kindness – that is, taking care of your body and mind. When I started weekday *Sunrise* I had to make some changes in my life. Being kind to myself through eating well, not drinking, finding exercise I love (like yoga) and focusing on sleep were actually the best things I'd ever done for myself.

Recently I hosted a body transformation and makeover show called *Bringing Sexy Back*. One of the cast was a beautiful mother of two named Sam (I know, it was confusing!). She lost 30 kilograms in just four months. That is an amazing amount in a short time – she had worked incredibly hard and she looked fantastic. She had a loving husband and tons of support. The only person who wasn't supporting her was her.

On the night we revealed how much weight she had lost, she broke down in tears, sobbing that she could have done better and that wasn't enough. She looked incredible. I was so desperate for her to embrace what she had achieved. Her husband had lost the same amount of weight and he admitted he looked fantastic. Women can be their own harshest critics.

Check yourself and know when you've done something good. It can be something small, like handling a stressful situation well, or something massive like losing 30 kilograms in four months.

Be kind to yourself. It's important to hold your own hand through life.

Setting goals: in a nutshell

- Identify your values.

- Be true to yourself every day.

- Create a brand for yourself.

- Keep your goals clearly in mind.

- Recognise when you've done well.

- It's okay to be ambitious.

- Make a choice to take a chance or your life will never change.

- Never stop taking chances.

- Be brave.

- Don't only remember the bad reviews.

- Tell the truth.

- Throw out everything that's broken.

Loving your body

CHAPTER TWO

I get a lot of attention for my figure. This sounds blunt, but it's true. My TV career means I've had to spend more than my fair share of time thinking about what everyone else thinks about how I look. If I always listened to what other people said about me, though, I'd be very confused – my weight goes up and down. I'm never quite right. The first thing many people say when they meet me is, 'You're skinnier than you look on television.' I take a deep breath and smile.

I'm used to hearing what other people think about me, but of course what really counts is how I think, and for me, being strong, fit and healthy is most important of all.

EVERY SHAPE IS JUST AS SWEET

We are all, thank goodness, blessed with different body shapes. I have girlfriends who are all the pieces in the fruit bowl: apples, pears, bananas and there are even a few lemons! My figure is quite in proportion. My frame is big and strong and womanly.

For most women, body obsession starts at a very young age, but despite going through the usual teenage worries, ultimately I'm lucky that I feel at home in my own skin, most of the time. I've had to stick up for myself so many times I now believe the words coming out of my mouth, and even when I know deep down I'm not quite at my best and could strip a kilogram or two, I fight for myself. Now I love my shape – I celebrate it.

In the following pages I'm going to share with you my body experience stories, the ups and downs and roundabouts, and how I came out the other end.

Young and strong

Even as a child, my body was strong and functional. I grew up on a sheep and cattle station near the New South Wales Snowy Mountains town of Adaminaby, 50 kilometres from the nearest major town. It was me, Mum and Dad and my younger siblings Georgie and Charlie.

There were no dance schools or organised sports. We had to make do, like practise high jump in the dirt. I envy the girls who had dancing lessons growing up. I never learned, as evidenced during *Dancing with the Stars*!

In summer we rode horses at pony club and through the bush. We'd gallop through Kosciuszko National Park chasing wild brumbies, trail ride around Lake Eucumbene, swimming the horses in the icy water before lunch and trying to help Dad with cattle work, but mostly just getting in the way. We had strong arms and legs and no fear.

Our winter sport was skiing. We raced for Mount Selwyn ski club and most years ended up at the Australian Championships. Now anyone who's skied will know it is no easy feat. It takes a great level of fitness and stamina. It gives you strong, powerful legs and a very strong core.

We ate for fuel, because we were busy. We took packed lunches everywhere (no takeaway shops on a 6500 hectare property), mostly white bread sandwiches with leftover cold meats, and we drank water. Soft drinks were only for birthday parties and Christmas in our house. Like many country women of that era, Mum baked cakes, pikelets and scones, although I was always more taken with dry biscuits covered with (I'm ashamed to admit) plastic cheese.

In winter we'd go off skiing each weekend with a mini chocolate bar hidden in a parka pocket in case we got too cold and needed a sugar hit on the slopes, but that was the extent of treats. Otherwise when we were out and about we got our sweet hits from apples or boxes of sultanas.

We ate together at the table every night – the TV would be turned off – and the meals were always traditional and simple. Dad would come in out of the paddock and Mum would have the dinner waiting: meat and three veg *every* night. My father would eat nothing else. He had a physical job and an unexotic palate. Now that my sister Georgie is married to an Italian, Dad has branched out into pasta and he loves it. But back then, we had lamb, beef or sausages, greens and potatoes every night, followed by a bowl of ice-cream slathered with chocolate sauce.

Puberty blues

I was the skinny tomboy who developed quickly at the age of eleven. My boobs were large like they are now, back then. Imagine the embarrassment! I was mortified when Mum bought me my first massive, ugly bra. I slouched terribly and she was forever telling me to stand up straight. I hid my body and tied jumpers around my waist throughout summer.

When I got my first period I burst into tears. My mum, Libby, presented me with two books she'd borrowed from the local library. One was called *What's Happening to Me?*. The other was *Where Did I Come From?*. She also handed me a pad from about 1965. It was the size of a surfboard and had a *belt* attached to it. What the what? Bear in mind, I was eleven in 1987.

Mum then informed me while she was sweeping the garage one day, 'Women laugh about these things, Sam. They even give it nicknames like "George"!'

'George?' I sobbed.

When I relayed this story a few years later to the girls at school, they gave me the nickname, Sanni Armytage. (Get it?) Thank goodness it didn't stick.

At thirteen I went off to boarding school in Sydney. In the dining room, a long way from home, we boarders would have toast-eating competitions and one morning I proudly ate thirteen pieces. It was over the top. I ballooned and at the end of the term Mum and Dad were shocked by my appearance. I blame my Irish heritage for the fact that if I even look sideways at a carbohydrate, I put on weight. And I tend to devour any form of starchy carbohydrate I can get my hands on.

At boarding school I was sometimes a little envious of the naturally slim girls, who seemed tall and elegant. I'm 169 centimetres so doing okay height-wise, but I'm not a giant. They were the ones the boys asked out. They usually had long limbs and most of them ate badly but remained skinny. Maybe it's just my faulty memory, but I recall they all usually had perfect, long, straight, shiny hair, too. They had names like Belinda or Erica.

Then there were the rest of us: the ones who didn't deal so well with carbs; the ones whose shirts refused to button properly over a straining bust. We had braces on our teeth, shorter limbs, freckles and mops of unruly hair. My hair is still so recalcitrant they actually have network meetings about it – hard to believe, but it's true! Every day I salute my hair and make-up angels on *Sunrise*. They are geniuses.

When it came to body shape, though, most of the time I was too busy to think about it, with schoolwork, sport, trips home for the holidays and more. I just got on with it.

Self-doubt, what?

Even after I started my TV career I still never gave my body shape much thought – other than how to dress it – until I appeared on *Dancing with the Stars* (DWTS) in 2011. My profile was starting to rise and suddenly it seemed like the whole of Australia was talking about my weight. It was awful, upsetting and a little traumatising. As I mentioned earlier, I'd felt the usual teenage angst, but all of a sudden I was experiencing something I'd never felt. Self-doubt. Was I fat? If so, why had I never realised this? Maybe that boy hadn't asked me out in Year Eleven because he thought I was overweight ... hang on, how rude! How dare people who don't know me comment on what I look like? I felt annoyed at myself for starting to listen to it.

It's inevitable when the media highlights us female non-models with words like 'normal', 'curvy' or 'voluptuous'. (Why can't they just prefix my name with 'journalist', 'aunt' or 'former greyhound owner'?) They then provide a running commentary as my weight goes up and down. Never mind that it might be affected by a relationship breakdown or because I'm just a little tired and stressed.

The internet trolls have poked fun at me in my larger times. Awful pictures of me in printed dresses will be forever available every time my name is Googled. With the help of an army of concerned wardrobe stylists, I have squeezed into all manner of control underwear and even corsets at work. This was a disaster as it just pushed my boobs up further under my chin and made me look bigger.

I shrank away from jobs and didn't put myself forward for opportunities at work because of my weight. I felt sick when watching my own *Sunrise* stories (not realising I was as big as I looked on camera at the time) and this affected my personal life; I felt I wasn't worthy of people's attention. I also slipped into that vicious cycle of not exercising because I felt so sluggish and then feeling sluggish because I wasn't exercising.

Then when I took part in a half-hour live radio 'lifestyle chat' a little while ago about my childhood, how I became a journalist, how this led to the *Sunrise* hosting position and more, I had just returned from a much-needed holiday and had dropped a few kilograms because I had been exercising, not drinking and not eating sugar, as part of my new 'wellness' routine. I was feeling fantastic. The (female) host asked me a few polite questions about growing up in the country before turning the conversation to my weight.

'You've lost weight,' she said.

I stammered, 'Well, yes, I go up and down but I've been exercising and eating well lately and I have to be healthy and strong to do my job and get up so early …'

'How do you feel about being called "curvy" now?' she pressed. Hmmm, the 'curvy' tag again. That's just a polite word journalists use instead of 'overweight'. Despite my confidence in my approach to being fit and healthy, this conversation just made me feel unsure of myself. As we left the radio station, the *Sunrise* publicist, Penelope, said to me, 'Jeez, Sam, I feel for you. You're damned if you stack on the kilos, and you're damned if you take them off!'

BOOBS, BORN THIS WAY

As Julia Roberts says in *Erin Brockovich*, 'They're called boobs, Ed.' Big boobs can make you appear larger than you are. My boobs have prevented me from running fast (yes, that's the only reason!), wearing shoestring tops, and men – and some women – stare at them. Slowly I have realised this is part of being me and I've started to embrace them. After I interviewed hot swimsuit model Kate Upton for her movie *The Other Woman* I thought, hey, boobs are really sexy. They're not something I should hide or wish away. (It only took me 36 years.)

You are responsible for you: taking charge of your body

It's taken me a long time to work this out, but there's something hugely empowering about being disciplined. After technically leaving home at thirteen, I spent the first chunk of my life (excuse the pun) with an enormous lack of discipline. There's a self-imposed syndrome at boarding school where you believe you're hungry *all the time* because you can't just wander to the fridge like you can when you're at home. Out of terror, you eat a lot when it's put in front of you. And given they were feeding a hundred girls in the dining room each day, what was put in front of us was generally not particularly nutritious.

Weighing it all up

In Western society, like it or hate it, weight (or, if you don't like the numbers, let's say 'how your clothes fit') is closely linked to contentment and confidence. I have only recently purchased a set of scales. I'd never weighed myself in the past – I probably didn't want to know the actual number – but I've come to the conclusion that it is valuable to have a set in the bathroom, because it's important to be responsible for myself. I should know how much I weigh. I don't have to share it – *in fact it is no one's business but my own*. Knowing my waist measurement is also useful: if I'm aware of where I'm at and the numbers start to creep up for whatever reason, I can do something about it.

I weigh myself once a week, only in the morning. I don't obsess about my weight. It's boring. If I'm not happy with it, only I can change it. If I have a piece of cake, I don't complain incessantly to everyone in earshot and then spend two days punishing myself. Falling into a vicious cycle of self-loathing is not healthy. I enjoy that cake, then take my dog for a walk.

I'm also aware of my Body Mass Index (BMI). You can find out your BMI on the Australian Heart Foundation website (www. heartfoundation.org.au) and whether it's in the healthy range. Keep it in mind, but use it only as a guide. I know some fit, healthy and slim women who are considered 'overweight' on this scale. If you're not sure about where you fit on the scale and how it works, consult your GP.

You are what you digest

As we all know, nutrition is fundamental, not only for general health, but also for vitality. I am obviously no expert on nutrition but I have searched high and low to find information in this area, so let me share what I've learned and my tricks. Find out what works for you, and seek advice from your GP and/or naturopath if you need more information. In my research I've discovered that the old saying 'you are what you eat' doesn't really ring true these days. It's all about digestion. You'll know if you have bad digestion because you'll be farting a lot (excuse me for getting personal but these are the facts of life), have constipation, diarrhoea, bad breath or bloating. There's no point spending time, energy and money preparing and eating healthy food if your body's not absorbing all the nutrients properly.

Think of the body as a high-tech processing plant. Do processed materials usually go *into* a processing plant? It's raw materials that should be going in, and this is how we should treat our bodies. As a first step towards healthy digestion, I like to follow the S.L.O.W. approach to eating:

Seasonal

Local

Organic

Wholefood

As a general rule, I try to eat wholefoods (organic where possible) – foods that are natural and not processed. If it hasn't grown on a tree, in the ground, come from the paddock or the ocean, chances are it will taste fabulous with all the additives, sugar, salt and fat, but it won't be very good for you. Organic food can be more expensive, so to keep costs down, seek out your local farmers' market or organic food wholesaler.

I walked past a blackboard sign at my local farmers' market the other day that read: 'Love food that loves you back.' Brilliant. The best bit of advice I've ever been given on food is, 'If your grandmother wouldn't recognise it, it's probably best you don't eat it.' Check the nutrition information on packaged foods and if the ingredients list is long and full of numbers, think twice about buying it.

If you're monitoring the foods you're eating and focusing on wholefoods, you should be digesting more of the vitamins and minerals your body needs to be its best. Visit your GP for a check-up and a blood test to see where you're at. I regularly have my zinc and magnesium levels checked. If these levels fall, my energy levels will drop, digestion will falter and I'll put on weight.

A 30 millilitre shot of chlorophyll (morning and night) also helps my digestion. It's available at health food shops. Also, Dr Oz told me personally that omega-3 oil is the BEST supplement you can take because it ensures optimum digestion/brain/blood/cellular health.

The term 'superfoods' may just be a marketing term, but there's no doubt they are highly nutritious. With plentiful antioxidants such as selenium and vitamins A and C, they are excellent for healthy organs, blood flow and memory. Try to include a few of the following rainbow of foods each day:

- Beetroot
- Sweet potato
- Broccoli – but anything green is excellent!
- Turmeric
- Cardamom
- Fennel or caraway seeds (sprinkled over salads)
- Chia seeds (in smoothies)
- Quinoa (an amazingly nutritious substitute for rice)
- Goji berries
- Blueberries
- Avocado (a great source of good fat).

When it comes to grains, I like to eat brown rice and rolled oats, because they are excellent for your digestion and high in minerals. Lean meat and eggs are rich sources of healthy protein. Packed with omega-3 fatty acids, fish and other seafood is also fabulous for you if you can get your hands on it. If you're vegetarian, legumes such as lentils, Borlotti beans and chickpeas are essential sources of protein. A small handful of nuts makes a great snack (try macadamias, hazelnuts, almonds, brazil nuts, cashews and walnuts). A drizzle of cold-pressed olive oil is a perfect salad dressing, and all you need! Avoid using it for frying as it has a low smoke point and will easily overheat and lose nutritional value. Instead opt for coconut oil, rice bran oil or macadamia oil.

For sweet sensations, try fruit (nature's sugar) or a square or two of good-quality dark chocolate. Cheap chocolate is full of artificial ingredients and your body deserves better than that. Tahini, floral honey and stevia are sweetening options that won't stress your body's delicate blood glucose balance.

I try to avoid white processed carbs (bread, rice, pasta) as much as possible – remember instead to 'look for the green' in each meal. Eating salad, but more importantly, veggies, every day is the best you can do to maximise your nutrition.

Healthy digestion tips

Clench your fists. Put them together. This is the size of your stomach. You don't ever need to put more food on your plate in one sitting than this. Portion size is one of the greatest contributing factors to the obesity epidemic. Try not to overeat. Listen to your body; when it tells you you're full, put down your knife and fork.

Chew your food – a lot! Try not to drink liquids with your meal, and once a week make water your only beverage for the day. We all know about the benefits of water, so I don't need to rave on about that, but try to sip, not skol, as much as possible, each day from a stainless-steel bottle (I avoid plastic as much as I can). Sipping water all day will aid digestion and skin health and, I've found, surprisingly, it fills me up when I'm not really hungry, just bored.

My morning routine starts with half a lemon squeezed into hot water, which is refreshing and good for digestion and liver health, and continues with herbal teas. Peppermint is yummy and refreshing. Dandelion is great for digestion and green tea is always easy. I avoid coffee because my mornings are pretty frantic and I need to get to 9am without the highs and lows of the caffeine hits.

Try a shot-glass full of apple cider vinegar each morning, fifteen minutes before breakfast, to stimulate your stomach acids, which will also aid digestion. Probiotics first thing in the morning will encourage healthy digestion throughout the day. I take a dairy-free supplement from a health food shop, but yoghurt is also a good source (check the label for the best levels of the 'good' bacteria). The jury is still out on dairy, but if you love it, have it in moderation. Some health practitioners now recommend that you remove it from your diet or limit your intake, but if you enjoy some natural probiotic yoghurt, reduced fat cheese and a bit of milk, go for it.

Bad digestion is also linked to stress. As in every aspect of your life, try not to be addicted to busy-ness. Take time for yourself, breathe deeply, set boundaries and make sleep a priority. (*See* Chapter Three.)

Recognise what is not working for you. For instance, I found that my 6am coffee (skim flat white) was bloating me so much each morning on the *Sunrise* set, it almost looked like I was three months pregnant half an hour into the show. I worked out through trial and error and many different coffee orders, with special thanks to our assistant on set who concocted a different coffee each day, that it was the milk. I'm not lactose intolerant – I could eat cheese till the cows come home (sorry, another bad pun) – but the milk was no good for me that early in the morning.

I would never suggest anyone should go without a morning coffee. If you love it and need it, have it, but try not to drink it after

2pm. Believe me, I work in breakfast television, so I know full well how it stimulates your mind and body, but remember it's a drug, and a mighty addictive one at that. Speaking of addictive …

Wine …

Vino, my dear old friend. We've been through so much together. As I've grown older, though, I've realised that drinking wine, like coffee, is best in moderation.

Even though we often use alcohol to de-stress, it actually has the opposite effect on our bodies. It's a stimulant. It has a negative effect on our sleep, as the liver struggles to process it and all the other baddies we've hammered into our bodies throughout the day. That's why it's common to wake up for no reason around 1am – it's our brilliant livers doing their darndest! On top of all that, wine and other sources of alcohol are full of sugar. The best drink from a kilojoule point of view is vodka and soda with fresh lime and I always have a bottle of champagne in the fridge because you never know when you're going to have something to celebrate.

The alcohol guidelines are now the same for women and men: no more than two standard drinks per day. Try not to have more than four drinks at a party. That's all you really need and remember, any more than that and you won't remember it anyway.

Being the drunkest person in the room is a really bad look: no one's impressed and they're likely to talk about you when you leave. Only have as much alcohol as you can handle – let it chill you out, not knock you out. Aren't your days off too precious to waste with a hangover? I'm starting to sound like my mother.

At one point I never wanted to leave a party just in case it improved. Now I save my wine time for the weekends along with coffee when I can savour it, enjoy it with friends and in my calm state I can process it properly.

One final word on alcohol; if you're not in a good place, if you're unhappy or feeling blue, be kind to yourself and stay away from the grog for a few days. With today's busy lifestyles and stress loads it very rarely brings out the best in us and it will only exacerbate any sad feelings.

Ciggies

After dreaming about a glass of wine, I now find myself thinking about cigarettes. I am ashamed to admit I, Samantha Armytage, am a reformed smoker. My first cigarette was when I was aged about eleven. I stole it from Dad's packet and snuck out behind the pine trees, where Dad's sheepdogs lived in their kennels. They watched on, heads cocked to the side, looking at me like I was mad. And I proved them right as I choked and retched, only getting through about a quarter of it.

It was completely silly but because my dad, my grandparents, several aunts and uncles and older cousins had smoked, I was curious. Then to be part of the cool crowd at boarding school, I'd slip off and bum-puff my way through secret ciggies as a form of rebellion. I loathed the taste, and it was ridiculous because we were all mad about our sport, training twice a day for hockey or softball or tennis, depending on the season.

Pretty soon, I was on a gap year in England and Marlboro Lights came in 'cool' little packets. I was an eighteen-year-old alone in Europe. It was so *chic* and everyone was smoking.

Then at university, even though I could barely afford food, I smoked. Again, because it seemed cool. I had boyfriends who smoked and all my mates smoked. By now I was well and truly addicted.

There were two reasons I gave up for the third and final time at the age of 32, and I'm appalled to say neither of them were to do with my health:

1. I looked in the mirror one morning and saw a huge new wrinkle near my eye. At 32, this is a MASSIVE drama. Since I've given up, it has disappeared, thank God!
2. I was the only one left standing outside restaurants in the cold, having a cigarette. All of my friends had given up.

Anyone who's given up cigarettes knows just how hard it is. I can only tell you my experience and how I kicked the habit. Every reformed smoker has a different way of coping, and each to their own. Patches and gum, for me, were no good. I do recommend you tell everyone you're giving up so they can help you. Also, while trying to quit, stay away from alcohol, which of course is good for you, too, because one usually goes with the other.

In the end I went cold turkey. I actually started the process by buying a packet of cigarettes, smoking one, then ripping the rest in half and throwing the pack in the rubbish bin. I thought that by punishing myself financially it would force me to stop. I'm ashamed to say on more than one occasion I went through that bin trying to find a hit of nicotine. When I recall those times I cringe.

In desperation I took myself off to a health retreat for a week. Cigarettes were contraband, so I couldn't get any if I tried. I had headaches, was in tears and was as cranky as a hornet, but at the end of that stay I thought if I could go without for a week, I could go without for life. I haven't touched one since.

My grandfather died of lung cancer in 2001. I'm relieved to say my dad's been in remission from cancer of the larynx for two years. Because Mum and Dad live five hours from Sydney, Dad stayed with me in Sydney during his radiation treatment, and if you're having trouble quitting, I suggest a trip to the smoker's unit at St Vincent's Hospital. The smoking-related cancers are about as bad as they get. I would go to pick up Dad after his treatment and meet some of his fellow outpatients. Some had the tops of their mouths removed, others had no tongue and many were smoking on the kerb as they waited to be picked up. Dad was probably petrified into quitting. He now still sucks on a white, plastic inhaler when the urges hit him. Whatever it takes.

Once you get through the pain of kicking the addiction you can move into a world where food tastes good again and the air smells fresh. And you won't stink. You may even become one of those terrible reformed smokers who lectures others about quitting! Haha.

Live a little

While good nutrition is crucial, I find that living life according to a strict set of rules is counterproductive. Life is here to be lived. Eat good food, try new things and drink yummy wine with friends.

I like the 80–20 rule: be focused and healthy 80 per cent of the time and cut loose the other 20 per cent. Don't forget all those women on the Titanic *who waved away the dessert tray.*

Please learn to love your body whatever shape you come in and make the most of it (as I'll discuss throughout the rest of this book) but don't get me wrong, I am not endorsing being overweight. The aim is to be strong, healthy and vital.

My weight goes up and down dramatically. I can be very hormonal. I have to work hard to keep weight off. I have an addictive nature and, like a lot of women, eat emotionally. I often eat when I'm sad, angry or bored, not when I'm hungry. I try to be aware of this and control it.

I do, however, aim to be the best I can be, to look after the body and life I have. So I aim to live a little, stay strong, and I almost never get sick.

> *'I like to be able to move my own furniture around.'* Cindy Crawford

*L*oving your body: in a nutshell

- Focus on being strong, fit and healthy.

- Ignore people who comment on your weight.

- At each meal, keep your portion sizes moderate.

- Discipline is empowering!

- Remember S.L.O.W., Seasonal, Local, Organic, Wholefoods.

- Try to eat 'superfoods' each day and search for the green in your meal.

- If your grandmother wouldn't recognise it, don't eat it!

- Drink water – it fills you up.

- It's not what you eat, but what you *digest* that's important.

- Own a set of scales – own it, girls! (Weigh yourself in the morning.)

- Avoid coffee after 2pm.

- Drink a maximum of four standard drinks in one sitting and if you're feeling blue, skip the grog and be kind to yourself.

- Remember the 80–20 rule, be good 80 per cent of the time, cut loose the remaining 20 per cent and live a little!

Keeping fit

CHAPTER THREE

I *have a confession to make. After a childhood spent outdoors skiing, running and swimming, excessive laziness at university and then into adulthood left me with a very weak, bordering on non-existent, core. Then, in 2011, I was approached to take part in* Dancing with the Stars. *It was a great shock to my body, not only because I had never danced before and didn't even know the basics, but most dance moves rely heavily on a strong core. I knew I must have had abs buried in my tummy somewhere, I just couldn't activate them.*

Over the next five months I attended dance training for about six hours a day and slowly, slowly they started to engage and then lo and behold, perform! It was brilliant. Gaining strength in my abdominal area led to not only weight loss but also better posture and a stronger body overall. It now gives me great joy to be able to stand up straight and proud wherever I am, sit down for three hours every morning while I'm on air without getting back pain, and do a plank, a sit-up and a push-up.

I aim to have a life in balance, in mind, body and spirit. I am healthy and strong, and my priority is not to be 'skinny'. These days I like to move my body and I rarely have a sick day off work.

Moving makes me feel happy and I enjoy the feeling of flexibility. I want to avoid being one of those older people who can't spring out of a chair and who struggle to get out of bed. At this stage of my life, when my alarm goes off, I bound out of bed. I love the mornings and I can happily touch my toes. I want it to stay this way.

As I mentioned earlier, I was incredibly active as a kid. My siblings and I rode horses and ski raced. We were into everything, but Adaminaby Public School lacked even basic resources. There were only 25 or so kids, but we made do. We didn't have a high-jump mat, but we did have the bar so we just jumped into the dirt on the oval. The long-jump pit was the toilet for many of Adaminaby's local dogs.

We ran cross-country races in the mountains and the air was so cold it would burn your lungs. We played tennis with wooden racquets on an old concrete court overgrown with weeds. We trained all year round for the annual Dalgety Sports Day, which was when all the kids from the district congregated and competed on the banks of the Snowy River.

We did our Duke of Edinburgh Award in the Adaminaby swimming pool, which at the height of summer got to about ten degrees. One summer I saw a red-bellied black snake coiled up in the cover and we all just kept swimming. We water-skied on Lake Eucumbene, and Dad rebuilt an old tinnie that we used to sail over the 'rapids' down the Murrumbidgee River. We rode our pushbikes and built cubby houses.

At boarding school a whole world of sporting opportunities opened up to me. I started playing hockey, softball, netball and tennis – on a green, manicured court, no less. We rowed and sailed on Sydney Harbour. I even played a summer of cricket in Year Eleven, although we only did this for the opportunity to get a tan in outfield and most certainly not for the love of cricket. This was a long time ago in a faraway universe where real tans were acceptable. (Again, I may not be young ... I have freckles and appalling sun damage now.) However, surprisingly for all involved, I turned out to be a fairly decent fast bowler.

While I am not an expert in the fitness field, I promise you that moving will *always* make you feel better, especially when it's done outdoors in the fresh air. It gets your endorphins flowing around your body and into your brain and makes you instantly happier and more resilient, therefore better equipped to deal with whatever is coming your way.

Exercise is essential, it doesn't have to be hard

Do you want to just 'get through' your life? Or do you want to enjoy it, savour it, be present in it and attack it every day? To do that with style in this busy, stressful life, you need to be resilient, and to be resilient you need to be calm and in control. You need to be able to make good, clear, rational decisions every time you hear that someone has been bitching about you in the office, every time someone cuts in front of you in the traffic, every time your darling mother is driving you crazy! Unfortunately, however, when we become either busy and stressed or lazy, or both, exercise is the first thing to go out the window, usually followed closely by nutrition. The aim is to use your body, get your heart rate up at intervals if you can (and you want to lose weight), breathe deeply and smile. It doesn't have to be time consuming or expensive.

I spend at least three hours a day in a TV studio so when I come off air I really like being outdoors. If you're like me and you *loathe* the gym, you can do things in your lounge room or in a park if you have a spare hour. It can be as simple as:

- Dancing in your lounge room
- Skipping with a rope on your apartment balcony (I have done this)
- Rollerblading is great fun (I have also done this – ON my balcony)
- Walking in the park with your iPod. Bushwalking is even better if you're near the bush (lucky you!). Add some hills and your body will thank you
- Riding a bike (with a basket) is cool: make it your shopping trip
- Tennis is fabulous although I always find it hard to find someone to play with
- Snow skiing is in my blood, remember, I'm a mountain girl! It's a great workout
- Paddleboarding is really fun and peaceful, great for your core, and they're cheap to hire.

I also love belting a bucket of balls at the golf driving range (*a la* Cameron Diaz in *There's Something About Mary*). You can do it on your own and it's an instant arm workout. It also gets rid of a hell of a lot of aggression if that's what you're carrying at the time.

Look for movement throughout your day. Get up and potter in the ad breaks while you're watching TV to burn kilojoules. Choose the stairs, rather than the lift. This is so simple, but I promise you it works. I climb the stairs between the four floors from the make-up room to our *Sunrise* office every day after the show. It actually makes me breathless and I consider it to be part of my daily workout. Try to get up and down from your chair in the office at least 32 times each day. Carry your shopping bags to the car, rather than pushing them in a trolley.

I recently bought a rowing machine which is sprawled across my lounge room (it has wheels so I can move it when visitors arrive). Rowing is an effective workout, especially for those pesky arms and tummies. Again it's also great for getting your anger out and it's not boring like walking on a treadmill. I keep two small (3.5 kilogram) hand weights beside the couch and do curls while I'm watching TV.

My mini home workout

A couple of times a week I do a little workout consisting of the five movements that are vital to your flexibility, strength and longevity as a human.

These are:

1. LUNGE – one leg forward, one leg backwards, deep lunge. Five on each leg.
2. SQUAT – make them deep. Another five.

3. PUSH UP – rest on your knees if you need to. This is really important for upper arm and chest strength and toning. Five more.
4. PLANK – I know they're hard but you'll feel so much better when you can hold your own body weight. You need to have a strong core, it will improve your posture.
5. PULL-UP – with small handweights. Bend forward and row from your thighs to your tummy. Do this five times.

Repeat three times. This takes about ten minutes. Easy.

Interval sessions

Try to incorporate a couple of interval sessions of intense exercise into your routine each week to get your heart rate up and burn kilojoules all day long. This means 60 seconds flat out and 60 seconds of recovery, for about fifteen minutes. This can be sprinting, hopping, skipping, swimming, side skipping – anything that gets your heart rate up.

Resistance training

Resistance training is also important for women – you need a strong skeleton to get through a long and active life! Aim to be able to do a chin-up. Aim to lift your own body weight. (This is on my bucket list!)

When I attended a talk on 'movement' recently, the group was informed that 'sitting is the new smoking'. Everybody's jaws dropped (we were sitting at the time). In the future, sedentary lifestyles are going to kill as many people as smoking has in the past and that's terrifying because, like smoking, we make a choice with what we do with our bodies. We should know better. So now is the time to get active and use your body for what it was meant to be used for.

Moving.

Stretching

Stretching is crucial for your body: if you don't have time to exercise in a day, at least try to stretch. Get a little routine going on the lounge-room floor while you're watching TV, focusing on your glutes and hamstrings, maybe a little downward dog and finish with some neck stretching.

Qi Gong and Tai Chi offer stretching and meditation, best done in the mornings to start the day with focus. My favourite form of stretch is yoga because it gives me a chance to meditate as well and give my brain a break from all the thinking. Pilates is really beneficial too. Find a good teacher, someone you can relax with and trust, and a location you want to go to, otherwise you'll make excuses and not go. Believe me, I've been there!

There are so many types of yoga. Bikram is great, although, beware, it's full on. Whatever kind you do, it's great for the room to be toasty warm as it will help your muscles stretch. If you're feeling tired – as I usually am, I often feel the cold – a warm room and the movement of the practice will warm you from the inside out.

I do Iyengar yoga, which is focused on alignment and precision, encouraging discipline and improving flexibility. I literally feel centimetres taller when I leave a class.

My favourite bit is the meditation at the end: I secretly love this the best and even though you think you're going to fall asleep, you never do, but you go into a state of deep relaxation.

Keeping a fit mind

So this brings us to my next point: meditation. Fitness is not only crucially important for the body, but also for the mind. In Chapter Four, 'Opening Your Mind', I discuss the importance of mental fitness and the benefits of mindfulness, but I do want to include a discussion here about mental fitness, as part of general physical fitness. We're being bombarded with 24-hour news and information, and checking Facebook, Twitter, Instagram, phone messages and emails round the clock. It seems everybody wants a piece of us.

It's a wonder our heads don't explode. Meditation calms the mind and it helps to protect us from all this over-stimulation.

For many years I was unable to do it, no matter how hard I tried. I threw my hands up, convinced meditation was 'not for me'. During one class I took I explained to the teacher, an experienced Sufi, why I was in no uncertain terms a hopeless meditator. I described how when I closed my eyes, I started thinking about the Dalai Lama. Then my active little brain began to wonder where he meditated and what his house might look like. Then I pondered whether he was a sell-out or not and because he was such a celebrity whether he flew first class when he jaunted around the world meeting Hollywood stars. Then I started assessing whether I would look good in his preferred shade of orange. And so on. Before I knew it I was turning myself inside out with angst and thoughts and my mind was going to ridiculous places.

During meditation I've also been known to think intensely about what I'm going to get at the supermarket after the class. As well as something nasty someone said to me three years ago. All the while I'm secretly opening one eye and looking around the room to check everyone else, convinced they are actually able to do it.

Then I found a good teacher who explained that it wasn't about emptying your mind completely. I should stop fighting the thoughts, he said. Acknowledge the thoughts as they come to you and let them pass by. Don't try to empty your mind, notice where it takes you and relax.

I started finding some of my thoughts, which might have been stressful in normal life, quite funny when I stood back from them and just observed my mind. I learned how to focus on my breath; what started really working for me was counting to four slowly on the in-breath, pausing, then counting to four slowly on the out-breath and pausing again, always breathing through my nose. This is all part of the practice and vital to good health.

To keep your mind as fit as your body, it's essential to take time out for mindfulness and sit in silence. Meditate a little and enjoy the present.

Try one or more of the following:

- Appreciate a beautiful tree
- Listen to music
- Read
- Sit in the sun, for a maximum of ten minutes a day. Make sure your back is towards the sun and your face is away from it
- Go to an art gallery
- Get up early and watch a sunrise

- Step away from the TV, sit still and watch a sunset
- Walk on the grass in bare feet.

This is one of the reasons why I love going to my parents' house in the country. There's plenty of grass and my phone doesn't work. Hurrah!

Check your mental health

If you think no one cares whether you're dead or alive, try missing a few credit card or mortgage repayments. I'm being flippant, but we all have moments of blue, and sometimes red. You're not alone – life is pretty full-on these days. Everybody's stressed and this can come out in different ways, including aggressive and unfriendly behaviour. It's easy to let other people's behaviour get you down. Try to be aware of yourself; ask yourself if what you're feeling might be more than just modern-day stress.

My grandfather suffered from bipolar disorder in his later years. In a small country town in those days there was no proper care for these issues and everyone just thought he was manic. Which, of course, he was. My poor darling grandmother was not equipped to deal with it and, God bless her, didn't really understand it. As a result, my family has been extra aware of mental health issues. (We're all fine – but we have our moments!)

Dad does a lot of community work and one of his 'off-the-farm' jobs is as chairman of an organisation called Riverina Bluebell, based in Wagga Wagga, New South Wales. I'm hugely proud of his work in providing a link to farmers and country people with depression. There have been too many suicides in country areas following devastating drought and severe flooding. These (mostly) men are tough and terrible at asking for help. They also spend great amounts of time on their own, which can be dangerous.

I think about my life in the city, where although I'm surrounded by people, I'm often alone. Isolation doesn't have to be geographic. This is why I think initiatives like 'R U OK? Day' are fantastic – although we should be thinking like that 365 days a year. Asking someone if they're alright could make all the difference.

Check yourself: know your body and your mind. Notice when you're feeling sad. If it's temporary, get out of the house and go for a walk. Better yet, run or hit some balls at the driving range. Get your aggro out. Ring a friend even if you think you don't feel like talking to anyone, and meet for coffee.

If your feelings are more powerful and prolonged than that, look at yourself in the mirror and tell yourself there might be something wrong. Admitting you have a problem is the first step, then take action. You're too important not to get these things sorted. Go and see a GP, and get help.

Dad once told me a story about a woman he met through Riverina Bluebell. She had been suffering from serious depression and had decided to take her own life. After taking an overdose of pills in her bathroom, her brain was beginning to feel fuzzy and as she fell down she grabbed the side of the bath. She broke a fingernail. She remembers being annoyed that that had happened. Then somehow she realised that if she was vain enough to care about a fingernail, she was vain enough to care about her life. She managed to call 000 and get an ambulance. She's now a motivational speaker and she has a powerful story to tell.

Try to find a person with whom you can talk about anything. It's actually best if this person is not a family member, a pal or someone who will blab. It's perfectly fine to go to a paid professional for a chat. I have a brilliant woman I occasionally visit who is like a mother, sister, employment consultant, priest and girlfriend all rolled into one. I call her my 'life coach'. She's my rock.

She listens to me, but she also tells me when I'm being unreasonable. She helps me to be proactive about things that might be bothering me. We talk about life, love, money, fame, working with men, working with women, my mother, my ego, etc. She has helped me change my attitude. She's helped me grow up. She's helped me through a horrendous break-up. She helps me believe in myself. She gives me tools to deal with situations. I adore her, and need her in my life. We think nothing of taking our cars in for a service, but it seems we're embarrassed to admit sometimes our minds need a service, too. I often go to her when I feel fine, just for a chat and to let her know how I am.

Sometimes things get so busy you might not even realise you need help until it's too late.

Healthy sleep

I have another confession to make. I am not, by nature, a morning person. As a youngster I was impossible in the mornings. 'Stop dawdling, Sam!' was my father's constant refrain when trying to get me out the door to school each morning.

I loved to sleep; I could easily stay in bed till 10am. In my twenties there was even a time when I fought my alarm clock at 7am, when I was reporting and had to be in the newsroom by 9am. Imagine the luxury! Now my alarm goes off at 3.40am and I can get an enormous amount done before *Sunrise* starts at 6am.

I'll often do a hair treatment, sing and shave my legs in the shower. Sometimes I'll make a smoothie at 4am (thank goodness I don't have a flatmate!) and then clean up said smoothie when the blender lid accidentally comes off and blueberries and chia seeds go up the kitchen wall. Anyway, you get the picture. I am now a morning person.

I have had to retrain myself. It's all about attitude and acceptance. Love the mornings and they'll love you back. Not that you'll probably be getting up as early as me – lucky you – but the morning is undoubtedly the best part of the day: the news is fresher, the coffee tastes better and it's the best time for your body to exercise. Try to see a sunrise (and maybe watch *Sunrise*, geddit?!) as often as you can.

To be a functioning morning person you have to be healthy. This means going to bed at a reasonable hour and having good-quality deep sleep. Every hour of sleep you have before midnight is worth two after midnight, so try to be in bed by 10pm, earlier if you can, and don't have any technological distractions in the bedroom. This means no iPad, laptop, email, Twitter, Facebook, TV, etc., when you're in bed. They're too stimulating and will affect your sleep.

I admit I have a TV in my bedroom, but I only really have it on to watch *7.30* on the ABC while I'm getting ready for bed. Then I turn it off and read. I find reading is the best way to send myself off to sleep and it's also really calming for the mind. Broken sleep is bad sleep, so try to avoid too much alcohol and coffee – it's shocking for your sleep quality and your liver will wake you up as it tries to process it in the middle of the night. If you live in a city and know the frustration of apartment living – hearing your neighbour's toilet flushing and your other neighbour's dog barking – try sleeping with a fan on so you can get used to that white noise instead.

I'm an extremely light sleeper and wake up if a car starts three suburbs away! I also find it difficult to sleep at my parents' farm because it's too quiet. Some people just can't be content!

Insomnia is the mind's revenge for all the thoughts you were careful not to have during the day. So you need to be as calm as you can at bedtime. If you wake up to go to the toilet during the night, try not to turn the light on – if you limit the amount of light going into your eyes you'll go back to sleep much more easily. Believe me, I know these things through experience, and a lot of it.

Sleep apps are fantastic and I urge you to download one if you're happy to sleep with your phone in your bed. (Switch your phone to 'airplane mode' first.) Some of these apps record how much of your sleep is quality and as a result you can work on what you need to improve.

Try to get eight hours of sleep as often as you can. I know this is difficult sometimes, but try to get at least six hours, worst-case scenario. I have hosted *Sunrise* on two hours' sleep, but it was after the Brownlow Medal awards night and it's a long story … Let's just say I invented the concept of 'Brownlow Medal Hair', which involves a messy ponytail that the Channel Seven hair and make-up department still use in times of desperation.

Napping is a great idea if you have that luxury, although never longer than an hour. I prefer lying on the couch because you're less likely to fall into a deep sleep. It's ideal to take your nap between the hours of 2pm and 4pm, and try to drink water when you wake up so you feel refreshed and ready to get back into your day.

Sleeping badly will affect your whole life. It will make you grumpy and stressed and potentially lead to being overweight and other health problems. It's vital you focus on quality sleep. Of course if you have a new baby, things may not be going too smoothly on the sleep front, but do the best you can to make your own sleep a priority.

Listen to your body

The human body is so clever, it will tell you what's going on, so it's important you listen to it. If something is sore, when something is tight, when you have a pain or a headache or are bloated, pay attention. Your body is trying to tell you something is not right. I have a range of health practitioners who help me and my body through my busy life, including a naturopath, acupuncturist, nutritionist, GP, yoga teacher, personal trainer and masseuse.

I don't see all of these people on a regular basis, just through the year when the need arises. Private health insurance can help cover the costs of these services, but if costs are a problem, consider your priorities. At least make the effort to investigate the causes of what your body might be trying to tell you.

Inflammation

Does your body just feel sore and sluggish sometimes? You can't put your finger on it, but something's not right. Watch out for *inflammation* in your body. I can actually feel it in my body, sometimes even in my joints. Inflammation is a Western lifestyle condition that can be caused by eating too much refined sugar and processed food, drinking too much alcohol, not sleeping well and not getting enough exercise.

It's also caused by stress. Stress leads to the release of cortisol, which is a hormone made by the adrenal glands. Too much cortisol in your body leads to inflammation (and belly fat!) so it is vital you manage your stress levels through meditation and exercise such as yoga.

To ease inflammation try to do some gentle exercise and improve your sleep. Increase your vegetable intake and perhaps decrease your meat intake a little. The spice turmeric is one of the 'superfoods' and is said to be super for easing inflammation. It's also an excellent source of vitamin C and zinc. I often add it to soups or slow-cooked meals like lamb shanks, and sometimes even to smoothies.

Some practitioners report that adrenal fatigue, when the adrenal glands are not producing enough or have produced too much adrenaline, is an increasing problem in women's health. It can be caused by intense and prolonged stress and causes fatigue that sleep cannot cure. As a result we often try to prop ourselves up with stimulants such as coffee to get through the day, which can affect digestion, lead to weight gain and even affect your sex drive. If you feel you need help, I recommend that you find a good naturopath. My naturopath, who is fabulous, has prescribed me Chinese herbs and supplements to restore my adrenaline flow. You can imagine how much adrenaline I use during three hours of live TV a day! Of course, a healthy diet, some exercise and quality sleep helps, too.

Keeping fit: in a nutshell

- Moving your body will always make you feel better.

- Sitting is the new smoking: aim to get out of your chair at least 32 times a day.

- Work out at home for ten minutes a day.

- Do a couple of interval sessions a week for at least 15 minutes.

- Aim to be able to do a chin-up.

- Stretching is crucial. Do it while you're watching TV at night.

- Don't try to empty your mind: acknowledge your busy thoughts and let them pass by.

- Focus on your breathing. It equals life.

- Be present.

- Be aware of your mental health.

- Find someone to talk to.

- Focus on quality sleep.

- Listen to your body.

Opening your mind

CHAPTER FOUR

*L*ate *in 2008, I travelled to the middle of the Northern Territory to film a story on a crocodile hunter. He was being touted as the next Steve Irwin. It was a huge, expensive shoot for the inaugural episode of a new flagship current affairs program coming to the Seven Network, called* Sunday Night. *My producer was a young guy called Michael Pell, who has since gone on to become my executive producer and boss at* Sunrise.

Michael is gay, flamboyantly gay. (He's also a close mate of mine and doesn't mind me saying this.)

On the plane to Darwin, as a country girl, I warned him to tone down his behaviour as we were about to spend the next week with some serious outback alpha males. He nodded at me but when we arrived, he completely ignored my advice and behaved exactly as he normally would. He'd just returned from producing the Beijing

Olympics and insisted on wearing his new Communist red Chinese flag headband tied around his head, Andre Agassi–style. He also wore his skinny jeans, his green and gold runners and talked incessantly about Hollywood gossip while telling our croc hunter how great his pecs were.

One of the locations we were filming at was an outback cattle station, which had a muster going on, so there were about twenty macho helicopter pilot cowboys there, too. As Michael continued to just be himself, every man on that station not only recognised him from his weekly gossip segments on The Morning Show, *but thought he was the bee's knees. For the entire week, they called me 'Amanda'.*

When we got back to Darwin I apologised to Michael for trying to stifle his personality and falling prey to stereotypes. I needed to keep an open mind like the outback guys.

Before I get to the fun bit about embracing opportunities and not missing out on life, I want to talk about the more serious, and literal, opening of your mind. These days we accept that we need to exercise our bodies to get fit, but we're still wary about exercising our minds so we can be wise. I mentioned the importance of keeping a healthy mind in Chapter Three, but I want to go into more detail here. Nowadays we need to manage our 'thought diet' and our 'emotional diet' as much as we watch our food.

One hundred and twenty-one million people around the world are now considered to be suffering from depression, and the World Health Organization recently declared that by 2030 mental health issues will form the biggest burden on healthcare resources, more than heart conditions and cancer.

We're over-thinking and it's killing us. Our minds are chaotic. We're wired in 24/7 and according to some studies we're checking our smartphones on average 110 times a day. During 'peak hour' that equates to nine times an hour. Some people unlock their devices up to 900 times per day, according to data New York–based app Locket has on its 150 000 users. No wonder we're all strung out.

We're constantly examining our email, Facebook and Twitter accounts, sometimes in the space of just minutes to see if anything new has happened, to see if anyone is noticing us, assuring ourselves we are indeed popular, and to stave off feeling lonely. We know everything about everyone else's lives, painted in the best possible light, of course. We're anxious, overworked, over-stressed and over-stimulated, so what can we do to help ourselves? It's essential to take care of your mind, and it's not just about lying by a pool drinking a cocktail.

Mindfulness

The latest research is pointing to the fact that 'mindfulness' is one of the key factors to a productive and content society. Since busy-ness and information overload are now such a huge part of everyday life, it's vitally important for your mind to be strong and resilient, and practising mindfulness can really help.

Around the world, corporations from Pricewaterhouse-Coopers to Google to the US Military and the British Government are now training their employees in the technique of how to be 'mindful'. Mindfulness is about zoning in, not out, and uses breathing techniques usually associated with yoga or meditation to help us become present and control our thoughts. It's about 'being in the moment' – appreciating your life and what's around you right now – and as with meditation, the idea is not to clear your mind, but acknowledge and manage your thoughts.

My favourite mindfulness technique during times of high stress, is to count to four on your in-breath, hold, then count to four while you breathe out. Simple. Concentrate on your breathing, lower your shoulders, straighten your back, be present.

As I mentioned above, mindfulness is not about removing your issues, it's about understanding them. Don't try to empty your mind when you meditate. Don't fight the thoughts as they pop into your mind, follow them, then let them float away.

> *Don't let your mind tell you what to do all the time. Remember to FEEL, not just THINK.*

Even though we own our minds, we don't always control or understand what is in them. Practising mindfulness enables us to acknowledge this, and brings a state of calmness and overall well-being.

In our lifetime, Nelson Mandela was the one person who steadfastly embodied the best principles of mindfulness. He wrote in his book, *Long Walk to Freedom*, 'Become the master of your thoughts.' His story is well known, but it takes unbelievable thought-control to transform from a rebellious young man, considered by his country to be a 'terrorist', into arguably the greatest leader of our time. Imagine how hard it would have been to avoid becoming poisoned with hatred after being wrongly imprisoned and tortured for 27 years. Instead he set goals and patiently held his line, controlling his thoughts until his time came.

Now to a completely different kind of hero. I probably talk about Andre Agassi a lot, but his book *Open* really struck a chord with me.

His negative thoughts were so overwhelming for much of his career, yet he overcame them in so many cases. He wrote about once taking on Pete Sampras: 'I can't beat this guy, I know I can't, so I may as well just try to give a good show. Freed from thoughts of winning, I instantly play better. I stop thinking, and start feeling.' Now that is mental toughness.

Very often, the only person holding you back from doing/trying/achieving something ... is *you*.

> '*We are all living in cages with the doors wide open.*' George Lucas

Presence

As part of mindfulness, there is real contentment to be found in being 'present' in your daily life. It might sound strange, but you don't necessarily need to be 'happy' all the time. What does achieving 'happiness' actually mean? No one is happy all the time, so constantly striving for this notion of 'happiness' is not realistic. Anyone who says they are always happy is either lying, or needs to see a psychiatrist.

When I'm being mindful, I try my hardest to be *present*. As Oprah (Oh Mighty One) says, 'There's a joy in being present.' One of my other favourite sayings is, 'Wherever you are, that's where you are.' If you're having coffee with a friend, be with your friend.

If you're on a date, be with your date. If you're with your kids, play with your kids.

Put your phone away. Besides the fact that constantly talking on the phone when you're with other people is rude, it's not good for your brain and you're missing out on what's actually happening at that moment in your life. I wonder about the people who go to concerts and watch the whole thing through their phone as they record it. Why are they doing that? Are they going to watch it back later on? Enjoy the music, watch the whole stage; hell, even watch the audience! (NB: watching other people dance is funny.)

On your deathbed, are your last words going to be, 'I wish I'd checked Instagram more'?

Being present means trying not to think about where you're going next, or what you're going to get at the supermarket later, or something nasty someone said yesterday. And if you wake up in the middle of the night, read a book rather than obsess over things that are bothering you. Enjoy that moment. As the saying goes, 'The darkest hour is just before the dawn.' As a shift worker with sixteen years' experience I have had a lot of practice in trying to savour that moment.

To be mindful, you need to be willing to go where the present takes you, even if that's difficult or not fun or hard work. Sometimes that can be uncomfortable. If you're talking to someone, be respectful enough to look them in the eye and listen to what they're saying.

I am often guilty of trailing off midway through a senten…

Whoops. But there is so much going on in my brain, especially when I come off air after the show and my adrenaline is pumping, that I have to try my hardest to focus. It's rude not to. If I'm feeling a bit scattered, I'll go off somewhere for five minutes to gather myself. The toilets at work are always excellent, although I have a colleague who likes to sit in the stairwell and regroup!

Try not to waste time and energy avoiding people you don't want to have a conversation with. The anxiety you carry around about this is far worse than just biting the bullet and having a short conversation. If people don't want to be your friend or they spread nasty rumours about you, or leak things to newspapers (in my case!), that's their problem.

'I will not let anyone walk through my mind with dirty feet.' Mahatma Gandhi

Take the good with the bad, that is the richness of life. You have a choice in how you live every day.

A healthy mind

Having a healthy mind is kind of like cleaning your house. It will bring you the same level of satisfaction, but be much better for you. Turn your phone off at night (unless you are using one of those fantastic sleep apps). Using your smartphone before you go to bed disrupts your sleep, depleting your energy levels during the day. You will be less productive and more stressed.

Avoid checking emails after 7pm. Because I go to bed so early I have to record quite a few TV shows, but when I end up watching them I often have to rewind large chunks and watch them again because I've been so engrossed in my phone – catching up on emails, Twitter and the like. It's not productive and not good for my soul, but I bet I'm not alone. I know couples who have made a pact to turn off their phones at night, otherwise they don't speak to each other, and some couples have even told me they text each other from opposite ends of the couch!

A weekly digital detox is important for a healthy mind. Try to have one technology-free day a week. Try Sunday, but if you really need to check your emails before you head back to work, do it once that night.

Try to get back to nature on your digital-free Sunday. Get outdoors, move your body and catch up with friends. Please make sure you actually *talk* to people and don't just have all your correspondence online. And as I mentioned above, take your phone off the table when you're catching up, not only when you're on your digital-free Sunday. You will be amazed by how good this makes you feel.

And if you think you don't have time for all of this try to take some time off Facebook, you'll be surprised at how much spare time you suddenly have. Your mind will be all the better for it.

Opening your mind to new opportunities

Opening your mind can be as simple as going with the flow, and embracing new opportunities to get the best out of your life. Say yes to invitations. You might be tired and going to a party is possibly the last thing you feel like doing, but if you have an open mind and give it a go, nine times out of ten you won't regret it. It pays to open yourself up to what life has to offer, and some of the most fun times you will have in your life will be unplanned.

I never want to go to a party, but I am always the last one to leave a party. As my Poppy Flannery always used to say, 'It pays to stay, because you never know when a party is going to get better.' Life *is* the party. It's always more fun to be out, meeting new people than to be at home on your own eating a box of Barbecue Shapes.

As you can see from my Northern Territory story at the beginning of this chapter, I've pre-judged a few situations in my life. I thought I knew more than others and I know I've missed out on some fantastic opportunities because I've been too set in my ways. You know the expression, 'To assume makes an "ass" out of "u" and "me"'? I learned this many times over as a journalist, and I advise you not to do it. Judging a book by its cover does not generally save you any time or pain.

I truly believe in trying new things and feeling adrenaline pumping through my veins, otherwise I feel I'm not living. I don't mean fight-club style, just challenging myself a little bit, or a lot.

I make an effort in my life to be adventurous, to be open to new experiences and to try new things. I gain something valuable every time. Whether it's being pushed off a canyon in a plastic garden chair in Queenstown (by far the most terrifying moment of my career); riding Octagonal's half-brother around Randwick Racecourse to do an interview with Melbourne Cup legend Johnny Tapp (they warned me he might bolt – the horse, not Johnny); hanging out of a helicopter over a croc-infested billabong in the Top End; or riding a jet-ski through shark-infested waters of South Australia for *Sunday Night*.

I like to think I will do what it takes to get a story and love the feeling of adrenaline pumping through my body. My challenge is to try to make sure I only use a healthy amount of adrenaline!

LIVE YOUR LIFE WELL

Listen hard

Laugh and play with abandon

Practise wellness

Continue to learn

Choose with no regrets

Appreciate your friends

Do what you love

Live as if this is all there is.

Life is what happens while you're making other plans. Try to go where it takes you.

Life *never* turns out like we think it's going to. It presents us with twists and turns, ups and downs. Hopefully most of the time it's much better than we imagined. But if it's not, try to make the most of it, and keep trying.

How did a girl who looked like this …

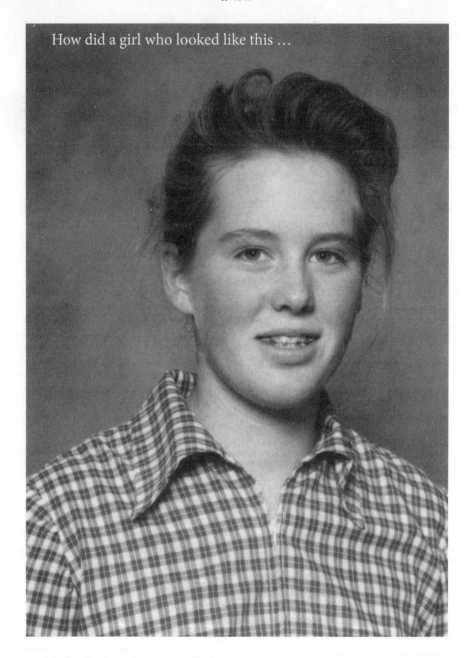

go to this?

When she really just wants to be like this ...

Try to be optimistic and enthusiastic. I love that line from the beautiful book (and movie!) *Under the Tuscan Sun*: 'Never lose your childish enthusiasm.' I'll talk about the benefits of playfulness a fair bit, so you'll begin to see how important it is to me!

informed person. If we were all a little more like this there might not be so much strife in the world.

Appreciating art

In his book *Art as Therapy*, British philosopher Alain de Botton says art can actually help us with our modern dilemmas, like how to alleviate feelings of despair and how to love better. There is a great value for your soul in appreciating art. Try to visit galleries and fill your house with beautiful pictures that give you pleasure. They don't have to be expensive.

My favourite piece of art (and the one commented on most in my house) is a giant prawn, drawn on cardboard in crayon and charcoal. I bought it for $100 at an art expo I randomly dropped into on the way home from work one day at Fox Studios in Sydney. I had it edged in white and framed in grey and I absolutely love it. It gives me pleasure every time I look at it.

So buy whatever art you can afford. It doesn't have to be a Ben Quilty (although I wish I'd purchased one of his brilliant paintings back in the day when he was an editor at Channel Seven, they might have been a little cheaper then!). My dream is to own one of Martine Emdur's sublime underwater nudes. There are so many wonderful artists in Australia. My mum is pretty talented, too.

The benefits of travel

I did a gap year after school, mainly because my HSC result was so bad I didn't really know what else to do. I also recognised that after my country childhood and teenage years in a tiny, privileged bubble at boarding school, it was time to broaden my horizons.

During my year off I worked (very hard) at a school near Bath in the UK as a sub teacher/dormitory mistress/jack-of-all-trades. I was lucky enough to meet war correspondent Kate Adie, who was visiting the school to speak to the students. Sitting in that assembly hall with the girls and listening to her action-packed stories of life as a journalist actually transformed my life. This was the moment I realised I would go home, apply to study communications at Charles Sturt University in Bathurst and become a journalist. But before it was time for me to get serious, I travelled extensively through Europe with a few schoolmates.

I cannot recommend a gap year strongly enough: it gives you the chance to have some experiences outside school and gain some valuable perspective on where you might want to go in life. I'm also living proof that you tend to apply yourself more thoroughly at university if you have a break after Year Twelve; many of my friends who went straight to uni were burnt out and flunked their first year. The gap year should be compulsory for all Aussie kids after they finish school!

During my gap year, among many other adventures, I:

- Slept on the ground at the foot of the Eiffel Tower
- Kissed the Blarney Stone
- Visited Amsterdam (the less you know about this trip the better)
- Danced in the Greek Islands
- Won a ski race in Italy
- Saw the Loch Ness Monster (I'm sure I did!)
- Was proposed to (many times) in Rome
- Got robbed in Barcelona
- Re-created *The Sound of Music* dance scene on a hill outside Salzburg
- Went to the top of the World Trade Center on the way home to Australia via the US.

My parents should probably never hear about some of the crazier things I got up to – they have enough grey hairs! – but my gap year was one of the best years of my life and inspired me for a lifetime of travel. Since then I've had so many more experiences through work and on my holidays throughout the world and each of them has had a profound effect on me.

MY BEST TIPS ON PACKING

As a journalist I have to go places at short notice, so I've become an experienced packer. The trick with packing is to have 'outfits'. Know what you're going to wear with what on a given day. If you just pack random articles you're going to get into trouble. This is why black pants are so handy because you can wear them with so many different tops, day or night, and the best bit is they don't show the dirt! Some people like to roll but I'm a folder – it works just as well. In addition to black pants and underwear, here's my tried-and-tested list of what to pack:

- Your favourite, most comfortable shoes that go with everything. A nice pair of sandals or coloured runners for walking/sightseeing/shopping during the day and a pair of heels for night (wedges are also handy because you can walk further in them and they're still dressy)
- Dresses are cool in hot weather, easy to wear and can be dressed up at night
- A pashmina or scarf for the plane and for cool nights
- A few singlets and t-shirts
- A blazer
- A pair or two of nice trousers
- A trench coat
- As many accessories as you can fit
- A handbag with a long strap that you can wear across your body; it's safer and it leaves your hands free for shopping
- A clutch for night time
- A roll-up straw hat
- Chargers for phones etc.
- A plastic bag for dirty clothes.

TOP: Mum, Dad and me as a baby in Scone.

LEFT: I always loved looking at myself in the mirror.

ABOVE RIGHT: Scared of the man in the red suit.

TOP: My Virgo cleanliness kicked
in early.

ABOVE LEFT: 'No, Georgie, you cannot
borrow this jumper.'

RIGHT: My adorable baby
brother Charlie and I.

TOP: My sister Georgie and I are still this close.

MIDDLE: My first day of school.

BELOW: All my Flannery cousins (I'm in the middle in the stylin' red pants).

TOP: Riding my childhood horse, Cinnamon.

ABOVE: On the stairs of our ancestral home, Como House.

TOP LEFT: Winning the showjumping at Dalgety Show.

TOP RIGHT: The day I said good riddance to my braces.

ABOVE: Last day of high school.

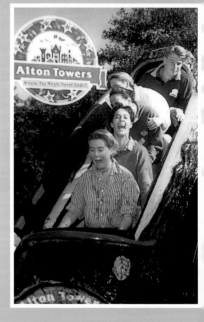

TOP: Post–Year Twelve leaving party.

ABOVE LEFT: Showing Aussie pride
on my gap year in the UK.

RIGHT: Scared senseless but still
loving my gap year.

TOP: Graduating
from Charles Sturt
University with my
mate Anna Von Clief.

LEFT: My first car,
'Ace Ventura'.

TOP: Dad's 60th Birthday — Georgie, Charlie and I.

ABOVE: All 'the family' at my niece Lucia's christening.

I've been chased through the streets of Marrakesh by a monkey, ridden a donkey through the Atlas Mountains, flown in a helicopter over the Grand Canyon, skied Aspen and worked as a reporter throughout Australia, Asia, Europe, the US and New Zealand. There are still so many places I want to go to.

Try to put some of your savings towards travel – the experiences will make you rich! When you travel, bring things home as mementos. If you think it's beautiful, bring it home. Pay the excess baggage – it's worth it!

Your home will reflect the story of your life and these mementos will remind you daily of your carefree, wonderful times. My house reflects all of my travels, some inexpensive, some I stretched a little bit further for: artwork from everywhere; a Greek goddess's head carved in stone from Athens; turquoise shutters from Vietnam; a camel's bridle from Uluru; Jim Thompson cushion covers from Thailand; even a snow globe from Paris.

Of course travel isn't all about buying things for your home, remember to tantalise your tastebuds. As Nigella Lawson (who I adore) says, 'There are many eating opportunities in the world.' The best meal I EVER ate was a simple Caprese salad (tomato and mozzarella) in a villa in Tuscany. I will never forget it.

Immerse yourself in different cultures during your travels. Try to use local produce; pick up a few words in the language and talk to the locals; visit galleries and buy art, even pretty postcards to frame when you get home; and look up – appreciate the architecture all around you. You'll be all the richer for the experience.

*O*pening your mind: in a nutshell

- Exercise your mind, not just your body.

- Manage your 'thought diet': you control your thoughts, they don't control you.

- Step away from Facebook, Twitter, Instagram ...

- Practise 'mindfulness' and remember to breathe.

- Remember to feel, not just think.

- Turn off your phone at night and avoid checking emails after 7pm.

- Try to have one 'digital detox' day per week.

- Make sure you have fun in your life and embrace new things.

- Open yourself up and go with the flow.

- Try to be optimistic and enthusiastic.

- Feel the joy in being 'present'.

- You have a choice how you live every day.

- Feel adrenaline in your veins every now and then.

- Read books, love words, appreciate art and architecture and respect religion.

- Travel as much as you can.

Being organised

CHAPTER FIVE

I am a Virgo. I share my birthday with Beyoncé, 4 September, just FYI … Virgos are the 'helpers' and 'nurturers' of the zodiac. They thrive on turning chaos in the universe into order and if Beyoncé is to be believed, we run the world.

The first Christmas present I can remember receiving was a washing-up set. The second was a toy oven. It might not be a feminist ideal, but I loved being a helper as a child. I was an ambitious homemaker and I treated my baby brother, who is eight years younger than me, like he was mine.

I might have created a reasonably successful career for myself, but I'm still a homebody at heart. My wardrobe is colour-coded. I order notes in my wallet in descending value. My car is almost criminally clean. My bookshelf is arranged artfully. My pantry is decanted into beautiful canisters (which may or may not be ordered from biggest to smallest). If my home, car and office aren't in order, I don't feel quite right. My mum was a nurse, so I learned to make a mean bed, complete with perfect hospital corners. I can't stand it when the sheets aren't done properly; I like it to stay tucked in tightly once I'm in. (I may be bordering on OCD.)

I have kept and filed almost every letter, birthday card, dress-up outfit, postcard, invitation and flower (pressed) ever given to me. I have even kept my retainer from Year Eight just in case I need it again. I'm not a hoarder, though, I am forever clearing out my wardrobe and discarding old kitchen utensils. I will even clean out a drawer at home for relaxation on a day off. Please don't judge me, I can't help it!

I have a magnet on my fridge that reads, 'Boring women have immaculate homes.' While I like to keep up a high level of organisation in my house, it's not always super clean and tidy. Often you can walk across my kitchen floor and get a piece of food stuck to your foot. That's something that would never happen in my mother's or sister's homes. I am the untidiest in my family. I know, I can't believe it either.

Most days there is a yoga mat sprawled across my lounge-room floor and right now there's a rowing machine there, too. By Friday my bedroom is a disaster. I will often throw things in cupboards or the washing basket when visitors are coming over and I have a terrible habit of taking my shoes off as I come in the door and leaving them to pile up in the hallway for what could be weeks. And large balls of fluff have been known to gather in the corners of my lounge room.

Despite the abovementioned bouts of untidiness, as I've said, I do know a thing or two about being organised, so I'm here to help if you need it. It's not just about being tidy, it's also about knowing where everything in your life is and being ready for each day. Don't feel scattered and frustrated because you're disorganised; organisation feels empowering and welcoming.

You can do it! It will take time and a bit of effort, but it's worth it. You'll feel cool, calm and collected, and ready to face the world. Here's my guide to being organised.

Life as a pie

As a first step, think of your life in terms of a pie chart. Divide it into several pieces and work out how large you want each one to be. Then try to find balance and organisation in each of these areas.

Your HOME

Aim to make your home a peaceful and secure sanctuary: lived in, not sterile. It should say something about who you are as a person. Fill it with flowers and photos and books, but try not to make it too cluttered. Chaos at home can spread to other areas of your life.

Keep your home clean and (reasonably) tidy. Know where your things are and keep them in good order. Be aware of where all your money is, when bills are due, what direct debits you have and how long you have been with certain institutions. Interest rates change all the time: you want to make sure you're getting bang for your buck!

Your WORK

Aim to make your work productive and contribute something to society. Remember JFK's words, 'ask not what your country can do for you – ask what you can do for your country.' Try to be a useful Australian and embrace our national values of fairness and having a go every day.

Be a good employee or a good boss, if you're lucky enough to be one. Do your job well and be proud. Be the sort of colleague you'd like your colleagues to be for you. Occasionally take a cake to work; it will surprise people. I take cupcakes for the crew from time to time!

At the same time, know when to step away from your work and take care of yourself.

Your EVERYDAY

Aim to live with passion every day and as with work, be the person you'd expect other people to be to you. Avoid complaining too much, it's boring. Try to be optimistic and enthusiastic. Have fun in your life, but know when to be serious.

Have a go at everything. Make a 'to-do' list for your life, and a bucket list, too. Think about how you'd like people to talk about you in your eulogy and live that way. Think like a politician and work out what you'd like your legacy to be.

MY BUCKET LIST

Write a book. (tick)

Ride a horse through the Patagonia Mountains.

Write an article for *Vanity Fair* magazine.

Do a flat-footed downward dog at yoga (almost there!).

Help young Australian women find their power and manage their body issues.

Own my dream house in the country, by a lake.

You can keep your bucket list secret – but have a few things that are simple or a little out of the ordinary, that you never thought you'd be able to achieve. Imagine the satisfaction when you do actually achieve them.

Your FAMILY

Consider what you want for your own family, how you might want to be a parent differently from the way you were brought up. Do you want to instil in your own kids the values your parents instilled in you? And how do you relate to your parents now that you're a grown-up? Family is precious. Never forget to appreciate them, warts and all.

Remember your values. Sometimes when we get busy it's easy to forget them.

Your EXPERIENCES

Aim to experience all life has to offer. I need to say 'no' sometimes so that I don't over-burden myself, but that doesn't mean I don't make a huge effort to embrace life. I know I'm not the first or the last person to say this, but I wholeheartedly believe that since we only have one life we need to make the most of it. Love, laugh, leap, run, skip, cry, and jump like a kid when you go to see that scary movie.

I'm saying all of this to myself as much as to you. I most certainly have not found complete balance in my extremely busy life but I do work hard every day to get everything sailing along smoothly, be the best I can be at work as well as protecting and nourishing my soul. Above all, I try to make peace with my imperfections.

Writing it down

Now it's time to get to the nitty-gritty of an organised life. I start with writing 'to-do' lists, they're one of my favourite things to do (yes, we Virgos can be very annoying)! I could not live without my lists. They keep me organised, so nothing falls between the cracks.

Feeling a bit overwhelmed by your busy life? Writing lists is the best way to get back on top of life.

Whether you write your lists on some beautiful stationery, or put them in your phone, record everything you need to do in order of priority, then cross each thing off as it gets done. It will feel so satisfying. Don't forget to be flexible when other things pop up during your week – just write 'em down.

I also highly recommend using a planner. Whether this is the calendar on your phone or a paper diary, use it to see your whole week at a glance and know what's coming! I have a weekly planner on the end of my kitchen bench, next to where I put my handbag when I get home. It's always there so I never lose track of my plans and commitments.

I know it's old-fashioned, but as our families expand it pays to write down everybody's birthdays in a birthday book. Putting them in your phone is an even better idea. My grandmother has 21 grandchildren (and now numerous great-grandchildren) and has a birthday 'poster' on the side of her fridge. What a great idea!

I often leave myself little Post-it notes on the kitchen bench for the morning so I don't forget to take particular things to work. You can also send yourself a reminder text – I sometimes do this when I'm on air so I remember to do something after the show. Set a reminder in your phone or write yourself a note. Do whatever it takes not to forget important things/dates/people.

Prioritise

Work out what is vital and what can be done next weekend. Today you must pay some bills, next weekend you can get a new gas bottle for the barbecue. Today you must get your online visa from the US Embassy, next weekend you can argue with your real estate agent about why your investment property has been on the market for so long.

Set aside some time to pay any bills and make all the phone calls you need to make. You'll find once you get started you'll be on a roll and it will be faster and easier to tick-off your 'to-do' list. Do the chores you most dislike first; save the easier stuff for last.

AVOID UNNECESSARY PURCHASES

Buying things just because they're on sale is not a good idea: you'll end up with more stuff than you actually need and you'll just need more storage. Ask yourself before you buy something, 'Do I really love it?'

Stick with what works. Buying every new gadget, make-up product or piece of technology just fills up your drawers and you'll probably go back to using the same old stuff you love, every day. Don't waste time and money seeking out the latest thing – love what you know.

Creating storage

Even if you live in an apartment without great amounts of storage (like me), you can create it. Storage shops and hardware stores sell everything you need. Hooks for wardrobe doors, belt organisers and clear heavy-duty plastic shoe and boot boxes can all help make your life more accessible and they don't cost the earth.

Label, label, label

I can't emphasise this enough. Use labels to remind yourself what's in boxes, folders and files, because you will forget. Don't fall into the trap of labelling anything 'miscellaneous', it will just annoy you when you're looking for something in a hurry.

Decluttering

Avoid having piles of things lying everywhere, it'll stress you out! Try to keep your surfaces clear and clean: reducing visual clutter helps lessen mental clutter. If your cupboards are in a mess and you can never find what you're looking for, it's definitely time to sort it all out.

Instead of sitting around, watching TV, find something to do in your house that will help you to be more organised. Schedule regular decluttering sessions. Spend a rainy Saturday afternoon cleaning out your wardrobe!

When you're decluttering, ask yourself the following questions: Do I need this? Do I use this? Do I love this? Will I need it in a year? Does it have sentimental value? (Keep it.) Have I used this in the last year? Will I miss this if I don't have it? If not, throw it away. Simple.

If you want to get organised in your kitchen, office, bedroom, bathroom, linen cupboard or garage and there is junk lying everywhere, first you need to be able to see what's there. Start by putting things in piles, then go through them slowly and throw out anything you don't need. How many of us put aside junk mail thinking we might take up 'an offer'? Recycle it! It's time to put things where they belong.

Room by room

Start in the bedroom. Take out everything in your wardrobe and drawers. Work out what you love and need and get rid of the rest. Regularly check your cupboards and drawers, especially if you live in a humid area because clothes can easily get mouldy – if this happens you won't just be throwing out things you don't wear anymore.

Knowing what's in your wardrobe makes it easier to pick something to wear to work, find something when you want to go out and pack a suitcase in a hurry. Put things in boxes. Give everything a place. Decide which clothes you wear most often and make sure they're easy to find, otherwise you'll be annoyed if you have to go looking for your favourite things all the time.

Group together all your dresses, trousers, shirts and so on. You won't forget what you have and you can access everything easily when you need it. Put your gym gear in one drawer together, your t-shirts in another, underwear in another (you get my drift!). If you don't have enough drawers, look at the options available at storage shops and discount stores. Try to find pretty drawer-liners and scented sachets to make your wardrobe a lovely, welcoming place.

If you have a spare room or extra storage, move your summer clothes out in winter and vice versa. It saves so much time when you're looking for things. Put your shoes on racks or in clear boxes if they're off-season.

Put all your jewellery in a box together. You can buy cheap, clear plastic sewing boxes at Lincraft that double as excellent holders for earrings. Have a nice jewellery box. It doesn't have to be expensive, it just needs to look pretty on your dressing table. Mine is bright orange and looks gorgeous with all my (faux) jewels spilling out of it. Clear out your bedside table and any other surfaces in your bedroom.

Keep your make-up clean and together in a nice-looking bag in the bathroom.

Go through your fridge weekly and spice cupboard and pantry at least once a year and throw out anything that's past its use-by date. Check your container drawer often and make sure everything has a lid. If it doesn't, chuck it.

Keep an organised linen cupboard, if you have one. Make sure sheets, pillow cases, blankets and towels are separated and folded and throw out any old or stained linen. I also keep a little storage box for tissues, toilet paper, toothpaste, etc., at the top of my linen cupboard just in case I ever run out. There's nothing worse when you have visitors.

A garage, a study or a spare room is perfect for keeping miscellaneous items you don't use often, but you need to be able to access easily when you do. If you don't have this kind of space in your home, a designated drawer or storage box will do the trick.

Group all your chargers and electrical cords in a bag or box and also your overseas adapters. Store your suitcase locks and other padlocks in a pencil case. Buy yourself a toolbox, so anything 'tool' related can go together. Buy metal shelves for your garage if you have one and try to stack everything neatly off the floor. Keep a drawer for presents. I keep things I can re-gift (ssshhhh!) or cute little items I come across when shopping so that when I need a present in a hurry, I've got one!

I highly recommend the humble filing cabinet. You can get them in really great colours (mine is turquoise!) from stores such as Officeworks. Create a file for each section of your life: bank, mortgage, bills, insurance, car, etc. I keep one folder for tax receipts. I just stick all my receipts in there throughout the year, then give them to my accountant in July. I know there are apps to help you with this but I still like dealing with paper.

Create 'folders' in your email inbox. If you're not already doing this, you need to start, today!

A final note on decluttering. If you're a bit of a hoarder and can't bring yourself to throw something out, try giving it away to charities like Vinnies or the Salvation Army, or sell it through websites like Gumtree and eBay. If you're not a keen online seller, you can ask a mate to help, and give them a cut. One person's trash is another's treasure. You'll be amazed what people will buy (a broken printer, anyone!?). There are free re-use/recycle websites such as Freecycle if you just want to make sure your possessions don't go into landfill.

The hand-me-down tradition is also still going strong. One of my older cousins has finished having babies and she's just given all her boy's baby clothes to my brother who's just had a son. Very kind and thoughtful and they're going to a good home!

TIPS AND TRICKS

Set up your phone charger at one power point and put your phone on it when you're home.

Keep your magazines in piles – only hold on to the ones you really love, and give all the others to the local GP surgery.

Keep clothing-store bags. They're really handy for carrying your dry cleaning and generally carting things around town. Re-use them as much as you can.

Hide your passport somewhere safe, in a place you won't forget.

Keeping an eye on your finances

Make sure your finances are in order, no matter how tiny your savings, and that you're doing everything you should be with your hard-earned cash. If friends have a financial plan you admire, ask them who they recommend, whether it be accountants, financial planners or insurance and mortgage brokers. Talk to your friends about who they bank with and what services they're being offered so you know what's out there.

Delegating

Women are generally terrible at this. It's all about trusting that other people can handle things and asking them to help you.

If they don't do things as well as you would do them, who cares? They'll still get done. Get a cleaner or a nanny or a housekeeper if you can afford it. Most of the women I work with – especially the ones with kids – have all of these things. Learn to say 'no' to things at work and in your home life if they are more than you can handle. People around you will respect you more for it and you'll have more balance and organisation in your life.

Tidying tips

Whenever you leave a room and go to the other end of the house, take something with you – don't leave those shoes in the hall, Sam! Try to put things away when you take them off.

I'm guilty of hanging jackets and cardigans and shirts on the backs of chairs. Always get up and do chores in the TV ad breaks –

like unpacking the dishwasher. Ever had one of those (premature) senior's moments when you walk into a room and can't remember what you're doing there? Yes, we all have them. Make them useful – do a chore in that room – like dusting the bedside tables.

Do as much as you can the night before

Getting up at 3.40am every day has taught me several things. The most important is that I now need to be completely organised for my day the night before. It's actually made my life easier, not harder, and it only takes about ten minutes. I put out my snacks (fruit, a bag of nuts for my handbag) and a cut-up lemon for the hot water I drink in the make-up chair.

I put at the front door my clothes and shoes and anything I might have to return to work, or will need for the next day. I keep my car keys in the same place, a beautiful silver tray, so I never lose them at 4am.

Shop online

This speaks for itself. Food shopping is so dull and a giant waste of time. If you've been spending too much time in the supermarket, make the change and order it online. Unless you have a big house with lots of storage, don't buy in bulk.

Keeping it all in perspective

We're all just humans and we all have the same number of hours in our day. Unless you're an on-call doctor, if things don't get done, no one will die. If the house isn't clean, it isn't the end of the world. You are still a good person. Just do your best.

Also, remember you can only be in one place at a time so if you have a million things to do at home, but have to be somewhere else, relax. Be present and breathe. Try to enjoy what you're actually doing at that moment. Most things on your 'to-do' list can wait.

If you need to, find someone you trust to talk to, professionally or just a friend, so that you can unburden yourself and get your head together – then you'll be able to order your mind and off you go.

Do your best to organise your life, but keep trying to enjoy it as much as you can!

Being organised: in a nutshell

- Find a balance between home, work, life and family.

- Being organised is about knowing where everything in your life is.

- Make lists.

- Keep your life as simple as possible.

- Have a planner and know your loved ones' birthdays.

- Keep your surfaces clean and free of mess.

- Don't buy unnecessary things, they'll just increase your clutter.

- Declutter and organise your space: know what you own.

- Ask yourself if you really love things? If you really need things? If the answer is no, get rid of them.

- Put things where they belong.

- Know which things you use the most.

- Store your clothes according to the seasons.

- Prioritise your life.

- Create storage and get a filing cabinet.

- Prepare the night before.

- Do your supermarket shopping online.

- Keep it all in perspective and find someone to talk to if you're feeling overwhelmed.

Living with flair

CHAPTER SIX

I turned eighteen when I was in Year Twelve (it was 1994, remember, as I keep warning you throughout this book, I may not be young!). When Mum and Dad asked me what I wanted for this special birthday, which was a very big deal as it meant I could legally get into pubs, my answer was a pair of knee-high leather boots. Fashion had not been central to my teenage life so far: I was at a conservative boarding school with a dormitory full of country girls who ventured no further than R.M. Williams ankle-high riding boots. Anyway, Mum and Dad splurged and bought me a pair of beautiful, long brown boots.

They were my favourite possession in the world. Well, they were my only possession in the world. We once had to evacuate the school in the middle of the night because of a fire; I sat on the grass downstairs for rollcall clutching my boots and my friend Jane took *her autographed photo of Wallaby Jason Little. I digress ... but you get the idea about how much I loved those boots.*

The social event of the year for most eighteen-year-old boarders was Sydney's Royal Easter Show. The nuns allowed us out for one night and we were in heaven. A group of highly judgmental teenage friends and I were getting dressed in the dormitory and I pulled on my boots, OVER MY JEANS.

I know! Hold the front page. From the reaction of the other girls you would have thought I had committed a cardinal sin.

'You're not wearing them like that are you?' one of my 'friends' sneered.

Everybody wears their boots over their jeans nowadays, but in those days no one did. When you're a teenage girl, you do what everybody else does, but at that moment I wanted to show them off. I held my head up and wore the boots over my jeans, and all night everybody commented on my look (negatively), but I didn't care. In the next few weeks, all the girls acquired knee-length boots and wore them over their jeans*.

---

* This is how I remember it, it might have been a coincidence.

'Be a creature unlike any other.' I can't remember where I read this quote, but I know it was many years ago and it has stuck with me ever since. Wherever I go and whatever I do, I try to be a 'creature unlike any other'. I know it's drummed into us from birth these days that we're unique and individual and it's harder and harder to be original, but you can do small things in your everyday life that will lead to a world full of beauty and flair; things that can make life just a little bit less stressful and sometimes more interesting.

Wishlist folders

Filing beautiful pictures in folders is my way of nurturing ideas about how I want to live. I keep three main folders, labelled HOME, CLOTHES and QUOTES. Then, like a bowerbird, I file things I like, such as paint colour sample cards (for houses I may decorate in the future); menu covers which have used interesting colour combinations; or lists of my favourite names (for children and animals!). Half the fun is keeping everything in beautiful folders. There are gorgeous coloured folders and boxes available in department stores and stationery shops which will look fabulous on your bookshelf or in your office.

You can also use websites such as Pinterest to store your ideas and inspiration online, but I do like beautiful stationery and to be able to hold the pictures in my hands. I'm a bit old-school in that way; I still use an old-fashioned diary!

In the HOME folder I stash mostly magazine pictures of beautiful homes and ideas for interior design. One day I will take a bit of each of these and build my most perfect dream house. I also have a few albums of photos on my mobile phone containing bizarre pictures no one else would understand – like a window I loved in a restaurant bathroom in Bowral and a heap of fabric sample names so that I don't forget them. Take pictures of flower arrangements you love, table dressings you think you would like to reproduce, outdoor furniture, pool designs, bedspreads, ideas with pillows, tree types, colour combinations. The list of possibilities is endless.

In the CLOTHES folder I keep pictures of outfits that I could wear and dresses I love, which is very handy for Logies time when I can simply give a dressmaker ideas and she can adjust them to suit me. I also collect hairstyles I love, lipstick shades I must have and jewels I dream about.

The QUOTES folder is my most chock-a-block. This is where I keep the material I draw on for inspiration when I'm writing, MC-ing at an event or even when I'm hosting *Sunrise*. This folder is slowly moving over to my computer, but as I mentioned, I do love having everything on paper.

Make sure you go back to these folders and boxes and look through them. Be inspired and use these ideas in your everyday life.

Learn how to cook

My generation of girls prided themselves on *not* being able to cook. As Carrie Bradshaw once said, 'I use my oven for storage.' (I have actually done this.)

Being at boarding school meant I never really needed to cook, so I didn't. In fact, every time I was home for the holidays and Mum was in the kitchen preparing food she would try to give me little hints, things like leave the avocado seed in to stop it going brown, but I'd ignore her. I was going to be chasing a career!

As I grow older I realise what a skill it is to be a beautiful cook; how lovely it is to take a gift with you to someone else's home that you actually created. I now ring Mum mid-meal to get her to tell me all the things she's been trying to tell me for the best part of the last 30 years.

I find cooking relaxing when I have the time and I'm doing it with love. Cooking every night is a chore, but I try to make it fun. It doesn't have to be fancy, just healthy, tasty and completed with love.

There are so many delicious things to make. My new favourite possession (although I still have those brown knee-length riding boots!) is my Tiffany-blue Mixmaster. I don't have a sweet tooth but if you come to my place for a dinner party, chances are for dessert you will get my signature sweet, flourless chocolate cake with hazelnuts, so easy and so yummy.

SAM'S FLOURLESS CHOCOLATE CAKE

Ingredients
150g butter
200g dark chocolate
200g hazelnuts
1½ tablespoons cocoa powder
6 eggs
200g caster sugar
1 tablespoon brandy
1 teaspoon vanilla essence

Method
1. Preheat the oven to 180°C. Grease a 20cm springform cake tin and line with baking paper.
2. Melt the butter and chocolate in a saucepan and set aside. Place the hazelnuts and cocoa powder in a food processor and process until smooth.
3. Separate the eggs, save 3 egg whites and discard the other 3. Reserve 2 tablespoons of the caster sugar. Combine the 6 egg yolks and the remaining sugar in a bowl and mix with an electric beater until the mixture is thick and pale. Add the butter and chocolate mixture along with the brandy and vanilla essence and stir well. Then add the cocoa and hazelnut mixture and mix to combine.
4. Use clean beaters to whip the reserved egg whites until peaks form. Add the reserved sugar and beat until firm and glossy. Gently fold the egg white mixture into the chocolate mixture. Pour into the cake tin and bake for 40–45 minutes. Let cool and serve with cream, ice cream and strawberries!

Years ago Mum made handwritten recipe books for my sister and me, filled with all the food we grew up on. Much of it has been handed down through the generations of both sides of our family. It's simple food, which was cooked by country women, with sometimes limited access to fresh ingredients – so it's no fuss. I love that my mum has added her mother-in-law's (Granny Armytage) favourite recipes, too; meals my dad loved as a boy.

I have jammed many more recipes and ideas into this book and it now sits on top of my fridge. Everything from ideas for duck-fat roasted potatoes to my sister's Italian mother-in-law's genuine Bolognese. (She is actually *from* Bologna, so it's dinky di!)

EATING OUT

I like to keep an eye out for new restaurants and I know my favourites. Having often been stuck when people from out of town or overseas ask for a recommendation and I can't think of any, I now keep a list on my phone. Then I'm ready to book a table if I have to in a hurry.

What wine goes best with what food? If you're interested in wine, this is definitely no longer the domain of the boys. I love that waiters regularly now hand the wine list to women in restaurants; I certainly accept it with gusto if it comes my way. Get to know the wines you like and which ones will best suit the meals you're eating, then check with the others and happily order for the table.

Fashion

Simple is best

In this busy life, simplicity is key. In clothing, home decoration, make-up application and friendships, and even hair and body maintenance. Try to choose the best clothes you can afford. An expensive purchase can be justified on a cost-per-wear ratio and it's nice to treat yourself to good-quality things you love. You work hard, you deserve it.

Aim to be elegant, not too trendy (I realise by using the word 'trendy' it makes me so not 'trendy'). If you like being 'on trend', buy seasonally at shops like Zara, Witchery and Topshop where clothes are much cheaper so it doesn't matter if they go out of fashion after one season. Save your money for the classics.

When shopping, walk away from something before you buy it. Go and have a coffee. Think about what else it will go with in your cupboard. If you're still thinking about it go back and buy it. If not, you've just saved yourself some cash. Avoid buying anything that won't go with at least three other things in your wardrobe; I promise, you won't wear it.

Being understated is always more chic and stylish. Don't try too hard. If you're lucky enough to have money, you don't have to show it off.

And always remember, never listen to the men in your life about fashion!

Figuring it out

If you don't already, get to know your style and what kind of clothing suits your body. What you wear is your 'brand' and people will judge you by it, particularly in situations like job interviews.

Be honest about your body. If you don't think your arms look great, no problem … cover them up, then pick your best asset and flaunt it. Legs. Boobs. Butt. Whatever you've got that makes you feel like a hot woman, use it.

Get to know what you definitely can't wear. For instance, I might love a crew-neck top in a gorgeous colour, but I will put it back on the shelf and tear myself away from it, because I have boobs and I can only wear V-necks. I love the idea of maxi-dresses in summer, but if I don't have a belted waist I look like Pavarotti.

Shapewear

We all love it – and there's absolutely nothing to be ashamed of in wearing it. No one needs to know. I wear it every day and some of the skinniest girls I know on TV wear it, too. My personal favourite is a Nancy Ganz slip for wearing under dresses or skirts. It goes under the boobs so it doesn't squash them down flat, but then does up under the gusset, so it won't ride up. It smooths out everything.

There are also skirt versions, which are great. I am such an advocate of shapewear I have made my mum a fellow convert. She had a scare early on when her Spanx 'rolled up like a venetian blind' under her clothes in the middle of a party, bunching around her middle. She had to race to the bathroom to fix it, but it was a beginner's mistake. Now she has the type that does up underneath and it's all 'smooth' sailing.

Feel confident

If you like the way you look and feel confident before you leave the house, you'll project that onto everyone who comes near you. People will want to be near you. Make sure you leave the house feeling like this every day.

To achieve this, you need to love everything in your wardrobe, with failsafe outfits you can go back to in a hurry, outfits you know are flattering and look good.

Wear it well

Try not to wear:

- Clothes with brands written across them (anything with the word 'Bintang' written on it!)

- The type of sandals worn by German tourists

- Clothes that are too small for you – the shoulder seams on a jumper should line up with yours. If a shirt doesn't do up over your boobs don't buy it. If you don't like going up to the next size for a piece of clothing to fit properly, cut the tag out

- Clothes that are too big for you: streamlining will actually make you look smaller

- Leggings if you're larger: they're not flattering

- Straps around your ankles if your legs are larger

- Tie-dye or cheesecloth

- Denim on denim, unless you're a fashion blogger or supermodel

- High-waisted jeans, again, unless you're a supermodel

- Elastic-waisted pants – you'll forget what size you really are

- Not too much jewellery: pick a few things – earrings and a bangle or a necklace and a ring ... but not everything from your jewellery box at the same time.

Try to wear:
- Good-quality, sturdy fabrics
- Dresses that are easy to wear, smart and flattering
- A belt with dresses – show your waist!
- Shapewear to smooth
- A properly fitting bra
- Blazers, they're always flattering
- Skirts at or below the knee if you're over a certain age (you will know what that age is)
- Well-cut pants if jeans don't suit you
- Pashminas or scarves, which can complete an outfit, even if you're just wearing a t-shirt.

Edit your wardrobe

Don't hold onto anything that doesn't fit you anymore. Give any unwanted clothes in good condition to a charity such as Dressed for Success, which helps women who've experienced domestic violence and/or relationship breakdowns get back on their feet and back into the workforce.

I have a rule that when I buy something new, I donate something out of my wardrobe either to charity or to friends or family. My sister, sister-in-law, friends and make-up girls all love this, as they've been the recipients of some barely worn and beautiful clothes.

Grooming

At work I get a lot of help from the make-up department, but at home I make sure I take care of my hair, nails and skin. It helps me look better, feel better and live with flair.

Hair

My hair is the number-one thing people comment on, both positive and negative. My recommendation is to find a good hairdresser and take their advice. If they do the right thing by you, stick with them for life. Amanda, who colours my hair, is almost part of my family: I've known her for twelve years and she probably knows more about me than my own mother.

Show your hairdresser magazine pictures you're inspired by. I often ask for 'Jennifer Aniston ash' when I feel like being a bit demure in winter … or I'll say, 'Take me blonder, baby, summer's just around the corner.' Even if you love long hair have a few centimetres cut off a couple of times a year to keep it looking healthy. It will grow back quickly enough.

Hand cream is great to keep a ponytail smooth in humid conditions. I love hairspray and use it a lot on air and off. As the fabulous former Channel Seven newsreader Anne Fulwood used to say in the newsroom on late shift when I was a young reporter, 'The higher the hair, the closer to God!'

A good blow-dry makes all the difference. There are many blow-dry bars these days and they don't cost the earth if you're getting ready for a special occasion, or you just feel like a pampering treat. These places are busy, though, so make sure you book early. Nothing you can do at home can compare to a professional blow-dry.

Nails

I like to keep my nails short and natural looking. I've had shellac painted on a few times, but I've found this damages the nail bed underneath. You also need to have the time to get back to the salon to get it taken off properly. Picking at it will ruin your nails.

Crazy polish colours are all the rage right now, but think about your outfit and who you're going to meet. The day I met the second man on the moon, Buzz Aldrin, the only words he said to me were, 'Oh, blue nails.' That was it. Not, 'Hi Samantha, great to meet you ...' The make-up girls had hurriedly put a fluoro blue polish on me that morning because I was wearing a red dress. I've learned my lesson about that: as my mother would say, there's nothing wrong with nude nails.

I'm sure Mr Aldrin would agree.

Save face

Cleanse your face well, preferably with organic products, and try to do a face scrub in the shower once a week. I recommend taking your make-up off properly every night: no matter how long it takes or how tired you are, it's worth it. You might like using toner, but I've found it isn't necessary, particularly for dry skin.

Find a good moisturiser. Sometimes it's worth paying a little more for the right product for your face. I have dry skin and wear lots of make-up at work, so I put four drops of rosehip oil under my moisturiser each night to try to get the moisture back into my skin. It's cheap as chips from the supermarket or pharmacy.

A great tip I learned from a make-up artist years ago is to use Bepanthen (yes, it's a nappy rash cream!) on my lips. Again, it's really

124

cheap and it's moisturising but not greasy. Paw-paw cream is also excellent. I'm addicted to lip gloss; there's nothing worse than dry, chapped lips.

Try to have a good facial every few months, especially if you live in the city. The dirt and smog builds up in your pores and causes breakouts and just leaves your skin looking dull. Exfoliation will help cleanse and revitalise your skin.

SPRAY TANS ARE THE BEST!

I have a spray tan session once a week in summer when I'm working. Nobody has a real tan anymore but I think a tan makes you look and feel better. Try an organic one that can be washed off after two hours – no more brown sheets!

Hair removal

As author Gretel Killeen once wrote, 'Be brave in love, career and facial electrolysis.' Many of us spend a great deal of our time performing hair removal. Laser is the best and most long-term hair removal procedure I've tried, although it is painful. Find a reputable, well-trained person to do it. The technology is so good these days it can be used on darker skins and the prices have come down, too.

Waxing is fine, and threading (an Indian technique where they remove the hair by running a piece of cotton over the skin) is really handy for those annoying little chin hairs – yes, we all have them. Again, it's painful, but worth it.

Tweezers are always the handiest thing in your make-up bag. And I love, love, love my magnifying mirror.

TERRIFIC TEETH

Teeth whitening is popular at the moment. There's nothing wrong with it, it's quite safe and sometimes necessary if you love coffee or red wine, just don't go too far with it. If your teeth glow in the dark or are too obviously white, it's not a good look. Take care of your teeth: floss along with brushing every morning and night. Good oral health will stand you in good stead, helping you avoid nasty, expensive dental work in the future.

Eyebrows

Eyebrows are really important because they frame and uplift your face (along with a smile!). Make sure you get them shaped professionally, and the thicker, the better. I envy the girls with the really bushy eyebrows and I love the trend started by model Cara Delevingne. Thin eyebrows are not flattering.

In my early days at boarding school I was bored one weekend. I sat in the dorm with someone's tweezers (I don't think I owned a pair!) and plucked away in front of a mirror. Plucking is contagious and like eating Pringles, you just can't stop. I took out virtually all my eyebrow hairs.

When I arrived home at the end of term, Mum nearly died – she had done the same thing twenty years before me … and hers hadn't grown back. Luckily mine did, but I learned my lesson and now favour the thicker look.

Make-up

As I said earlier I wear a lot of make-up for work, so I don't wear much in my 'real life', much to my mother's annoyance. She likes me to 'put some lipstick on' just to go into town to get milk. I'm more than happy to go *au naturel*.

When I do have to do my own make-up, I use a really natural foundation (like Chanel Lumière) and I always apply it with a brush. People tell me how good my skin is, but it's the foundation that is dewy and makes my skin look better than it is. (Fake it till you make it, girls!)

I use a crème blush (MAC), again, because it's dewy and I love pink cheeks and lips. I also use mascara (ModelCo) and have tried every brand on the market. Most of them are terrible. Give me a straight brush and mascara that doesn't slide down your face and I'll be happy!

Sometimes I'll get eyelash extensions if I'm going away on holidays but, like shellac on your nails, it does harm your natural lashes so do it sparingly and don't make them too long, otherwise you'll look like Bambi. Try not to make them too obvious: just thicker than normal is fine.

Ageing gracefully

Each year as our birthdays roll around, my Channel Seven girlfriends and I do the usual complaining about being another year older and creakier over champagne. As we always say, TV years are like dog years. One member of this group is the divine Sally Obermeder, who battled and beat breast cancer in 2012. Sal always pulls us up and reminds us that if we're still having birthdays, we're lucky. I couldn't agree more.

The changes that come with growing older are not always fun. I'm at that point in my life when I'm getting wrinkles and yet, still getting pimples! Despite this conundrum, I do my best to make sure my ageing is as healthy as possible.

I'm not going to lie to you, getting up early for my work is tiring. When I got the *Sunrise* job I realised I didn't want to let the weariness rule my life, so I made a conscious decision to do everything I could to manage my lifestyle. Not only do I want to look good for my age, I want to feel young in my mind and my spirit. I want to be healthy and vital and to be a good daughter, sister, friend, cousin, niece and aunt.

Growing older and more tired is scary, especially for women, but there is a way to do it gracefully. I work hard to maintain my energy levels and get enough sleep. I take care of my skin, my nutrition, my hydration, I've cut down on alcohol and I don't smoke. Smiling and laughing helps, even when I don't feel like it. In fact, *especially* then. If I'm particularly tired and irritated and think I might snap at someone close to me, silence is always the best option.

Exercise is excellent for keeping you young. Maintain a regular exercise regimen, choosing activities that will enhance your strength, endurance and cardiovascular fitness.

I've become more comfortable in my skin as I've aged. I feel much more attractive and together now than I felt at 21. There's the saying, 'Youth is wasted on the young.' Well I wouldn't go back to my twenties for anything. I'm having far too much fun now.

As you grow older you can contribute to society in a more positive and productive way. You don't care what other people think of you so much and you trust your instincts more. You often have a better haircut, too.

I don't agree with fighting the ageing process. Be the best you can be for your age. If you're 38 (like me) don't try to look 25, look good for 38! (Actually I tell people I'm 75, so they think I look *really* good for my age.)

As we all grow older, we're all dealing with it as best we can.

Sometimes I just can't help but stare at some people's faces, when they go too far with surgery, botox and fillers. Give me a worn-in, expressive face any day.

Of course, though, each to their own.

Being playful

Being playful definitely keeps me young at heart. Sometimes I get into trouble for this from other media outlets, but I simply refuse to take myself seriously. I firmly believe playfulness is one of the major childhood traits we should bring with us into adulthood – and yet so many of us think we're too old or too cool to play. I just love being silly.

- I love sitting on the floor
- I love running and skipping (even though I'm slightly uncoordinated)
- I love singing loudly (even though I'm tone deaf)
- I will always stop and jump on a child's swing in a park
- I still love jumping on trampolines
- I love silly-dancing with my niece in the lounge room (she refers to 'Happy' by Pharrell Williams as 'Auntie Sammy's song').

I have a greeting card stuck on my fridge which I look at every day. It reads: *Be honest, be kind, be silly.* I try my best to fit these three things into every one of my days. (I also have a card on my fridge that reads: *It's better to have loved and lost than to live with the psycho for the rest of your life*, but that's for another chapter.)

Being silly and playful will keep you young at heart and spread positivity and joy through all areas of your life. You will shine and glow with life and vitality.

Being grateful

Being grateful makes us happy. Sometimes we lose sight of the fact that we have wonderful, safe lives here in Australia. I try not to think about what I don't have, what I've missed out on, what went wrong. I remind myself about what I *do* have and how lucky I am.

All of this will help you to live with flair. If you love yourself first, take pride in your appearance and are not bitter about what other people have, you will be great company – people will gravitate towards you. Remember, many people's lives aren't as great as they might look from the outside. Everyone has their crosses to bear. Be happy with your lot and if you really don't like something, change it if it is within your power.

And if those around you are enjoying successful lives, be happy for them. The true sign of a happy person is one who can be pleased for the good fortune of others.

Speaking in public

Embrace public speaking. Some of the best speeches I've ever heard were at country weddings, not by professionals, but by people who were genuine, spoke from the heart and used really touching words. Being able to speak confidently in public is such a great skill and people should hear what you have to say. I love it when brides speak at their own weddings, although in my experience many of them are too shy and still let their father and husbands speak on their behalf. They might actually enjoy having their say on their big day.

I still get nervous when speaking in public; it's much easier for me to sit in front of a camera than stand in front of a room full of people who will react, sometimes not positively! If you're going to make a speech or a presentation and you're nervous, try the following tips.

- Make sure you're prepared – know your stuff. I appear in public often as part of my work and I always use notes. It's a certain skill to be able to talk off the cuff at length – usually one honed by politicians

- Make eye contact – people will connect with you and warm to what you're saying if you look them in the eye
- Be yourself; talk to people like you would talk to your mates over a coffee or a glass of wine
- Take a risk – people are generally forgiving of public speakers. Sometimes I've wondered if a joke would go down well, considered dropping it, then run with it anyway. Usually those lines are the hit of the speech
- Know your audience – I was recently at a lunch for 800 networking women and a male comedian was the main act. His performance was the crudest and rudest I've ever heard. It was cringeworthy. No one laughed. He was probably better suited to a football club locker room.

I was once given a useful chart by a former colleague, which is probably made up, but I always go back to it when I'm preparing to speak in public. The advice she gave was:

When you're addressing a group of people, be it socially or in the office, it pays to remember –

- 25 per cent are listening

- 12 per cent will understand what is said

- 4 per cent will be able to recall what was said

- 11 per cent will have switched off altogether

- 48 per cent are thinking about what they will be doing when the function finishes.

Keeping all this in mind will give you confidence, even if it's made up. (I'm sure it's at least partly true!)

BE KIND TO YOURSELF

If you're going to live with flair, you need to be nice to yourself. That means knowing things like when to have an early night, when to have an alcohol-free night and going for a walk in the fresh air to make your body strong when you're so exhausted you just want to lie on the lounge.

Fill your body with healthy, organic food so it is better equipped to carry you around all day. Swap your heels for flats, even if just for one day, to give your poor, battered feet a rest.

You make a choice to be kind to yourself. When you self-sabotage, you only hurt yourself.

Being kind to others

A little bit of karma goes a long way. If you still have time left on your parking ticket, jump out of your car and hand it to the person waiting behind to pull into your spot. I often do this and it's hilarious to see annoyance turn to gratitude when the driver realises you're holding them up to help them.

I love chatting to people in the post office queue and the grumpier they are, the better. It's a little challenge I set myself, to see if I can change a stranger's mood. While country people are, as a rule, friendly and happy to chat at any time, people in the city are usually surprised when a complete stranger strikes up a conversation. They often relax and start talking back and if they seemed grumpy at first, you discover that they're actually quite nice. Maybe they were just having a bad day.

If you walk past someone you know in the street, say 'hi', even if you don't particularly like them or there is some sort of awkwardness between you. It's not hard to say a quick 'hi' and keep walking, and it makes you feel connected to your fellow human beings. Rushing past with your head down won't give you the same good feelings.

Compliment people, it puts them off guard. (I'm joking, of course.) Compliment people with sincerity because it's a good thing to do all round. Try to give one compliment a day. If you think something nice, communicate it to that person. Too often I think something positive about someone but don't pass it on. I'm trying to train myself to say it out loud.

Years ago when I was a political correspondent for *Sky News* I was working in the bureau in Canberra, quite disconnected from the main studio in Sydney. I was doing my best and working like a dog, but not really getting any feedback. One day out of the blue, I received an email from one of the senior presenters in Sydney, Leigh Hatcher. Leigh is a highly experienced journalist and an excellent newsreader, but more than that, he's a lovely man. In his email he said he'd been thinking about what a great job I'd been doing, how delightful it was to cross to me and how much he enjoyed our chats down the line. He said he'd wanted to express his thoughts to me for a while, but wanted to write them down. This profoundly touched me. I printed out the email and put it in a special box where I keep all the correspondence that is precious to me.

It was a simple thing to do. People in senior positions in any industry can forget how huge a few small words of encouragement can be. Leigh's words spurred me on to continue on my path.

How people treat others is a measure of their character. When I dine with people I don't know too well – new friends, potential boyfriends, work colleagues – I always find it fascinating to watch how they treat the restaurant wait staff. I can quickly sum up someone's moral character by observing their behaviour in this situation.

136

There is no bigger turn-off than people who are rude to waiters, other than maybe people who wave their knife around while eating and talking, or people who get so drunk they fall off their chair and you have to put yourself in a taxi and go home … (Both these things have happened to me on dates.)

Apart from treating waiters with respect, I always leave at least a 10 per cent tip. Many of them are at university, and one day you might be working for them. I waitressed during my university days and as my mother often says, 'Always be nice to the last person who touches your food.'

*L*iving with flair: in a nutshell

- Keep folders, on paper or online, of pictures and words that inspire you.

- Know how to cook well and be able to handle the wine list.

- Simple and stylish is best, avoid being flashy.

- Pick your best asset and flaunt it; hide what you don't like so much.

- Shapewear is FABULOUS.

- Be a creature unlike any other.

- Find a good hairdresser.

- Try to have a good facial every few months – especially if you live in a city.

- Don't do anything in your beauty routine that looks obvious.

- Take care of your eyebrows – they frame your face!

- Ageing is a privilege.

- 'Playing' makes you feel young.

- Be grateful for what you *do* have.

- Embrace speaking in public.

- Be kind to yourself.

- If you think something nice and supportive about another person, say it to them.

- Talk to strangers.

Rising above it

CHAPTER SEVEN

As I mentioned at the beginning of Chapter Two, my job means I'm an easy target for negative attention and behaviour. This can be hard, so I've had to work out an approach to life that involves staying positive, looking for the best in every situation, and rising above it.

This has been a bit of a rocky road. Years ago, just after I was promoted to host Weekend Sunrise, *I was invited to a dinner party. I was with my then boyfriend and the people at the table were his friends. Some people can be a little edgy around TV 'personalities'. They expect TV people to be egomaniacs who are completely out of touch with the average Australian. Sometimes they're right, but on the whole we're just hardworking Aussies doing a job. I like to quietly change people's attitudes.*

At the beginning of the night the other dinner guests variously told me things like they'd never seen my work before or they didn't own a television. Or they said, 'I only ever watch the ABC, I don't bother with the commercial networks.' One of my aunts still tells me this every time I see her.

As the night wore on everything changed. 'You wore a tan blazer two weeks ago and I loved it, where can I get one?' one woman asked me three wine-fuelled hours after telling me she'd never seen me before.

'You're slimmer and prettier in real life,' a bloke informed me after many beers.

'You interviewed Kevin Rudd last weekend and you let him get away with murder,' another volunteered. He was the one who said he didn't own a TV. I have to steel myself and rise above it because all of this is part-and-parcel of my job.

It's a difficult lesson to learn, being the 'bigger person'. It's meant to be so rewarding, but often it doesn't feel like that. This was the number-one belief drummed into me in my childhood.

Sometimes being the bigger person means smiling and walking away, while fantasising about punching the other person in the throat.

Ultimately I know that this is the best way to deal with negative situations.

My sixteen-year-old self is still there, though, just below the surface. Every time someone says something mean, every time another woman is nasty towards me, every time someone copies me, follows me, annoys me, I try to rise above it. Rising above it is the healthiest thing to do. It's also the most stylish. When people are nasty, unkind, rude to you, gossip about you (or leak things to newspapers), rise above it.

No one is immune to this: I once read an interview with supermodel Gisele Bündchen in which she said she couldn't work out why she didn't have any female friends.

In these times of enormous stress and busy-ness and excessive criticism, particularly on social media, when people are being more awful to others than ever before, it's becoming increasingly harder to stay optimistic.

My guide to staying cool

- Unless you're giving birth, let people pass you in queues or in traffic. It may just give you a warm feeling about your fellow humans. I live in Sydney, Australia's biggest city, and I'm constantly appalled at other drivers, especially when it comes to emergency vehicles. Drivers don't pull over regularly these days to let ambulances pass and if they do, it's galling to see how many duck in directly after the ambulance to try to make the traffic light. Patience is a virtue, as the saying goes. I feel a lot less stressed if I make room for other drivers.

- Occasionally let the other person be right in an argument. You don't have to 'win' every time.

- Richard Carlson, the author of *Don't Sweat the Small Stuff*, wrote, 'Choose to be kind rather than be right in an argument.' Especially in a petty argument, be the better person, particularly if there's alcohol involved. You'll feel better in the end.

- Be happy for others when good things happen in their lives. There are so many jealous people out there. Be the one who's not.

- Walk away from conflict. This doesn't mean you're weak or scared, it means the situation isn't worth your important energy. Be kind to yourself. Tell your ego to cool it. Ego is the only requirement to destroy any relationship.

- Let people be. Live and let live. If your partner wants to break up and date someone else, let them go, otherwise you're just making a fool of yourself. Life is not a soap opera (although it can sometimes feel like one!). You cannot force someone to love you and I promise it will always work out for the best. That guy you think is so wonderful and the only person for you in the world right now may turn out to be a bald alcoholic in 40 years' time. Be thankful: you may have dodged a bullet.

- Do something nice for someone and don't expect anything in return. Pay people compliments: everyone likes attention and praise. Do the chores, even if it isn't your turn. It saves a lot of pain to realise you're not always going to be appreciated or receive something in return every time you do something good for someone else.

- Change your plans if you're asked to, and be happy to do it. It's important to be flexible, otherwise you'll drive yourself nuts.

- Occasionally admit you're wrong, even when you think you're right. Humans always think they're right. Nothing shuts a conversation up faster than saying, 'I apologise. I had it wrong.' If for nothing else, do it to surprise people.

- Try not to play tit for tat. If you feel like you're a better friend to someone than they are to you, let it go. You never know everything about other people's lives, and they may not be in the position to be the best kind of friend at the moment.

- Accept that people aren't perfect and will inevitably behave in ways that won't always please you. How many times have you said to someone, 'I would never have behaved like that'? If someone takes your job, your boyfriend, cancels plans, doesn't behave as you think they should, get over it.

- Don't take criticism personally. No one is perfect. It's under-standable we don't like having our flaws pointed out to us, but criticism is part of life. Think of it as 'commentary' (I get a lot of this!) and you can't control what other people say about you. Ignore it and live your life. It's not important what other people think of you – what's important comes from inside.

Be the bigger person, skip the 'e' and let it 'go'.

Nasty people: why do they do it?

It pays to keep in mind what drives nasty and unkind people, then you can walk away from them and, most importantly, not let their words or actions sting. There are a lot of quotes and sayings that I keep in mind in these situations. One of them is, 'Be kind to unkind people – they need it the most.' I really believe this. Negative, nasty behaviours usually come from a negative place within.

What is that negative place within? What drives nasty people? Usually it's jealousy. Think back to the things your mother has said to you over the years. Perhaps it was about that girl at primary school who was mean to you – was she just jealous? Well, guess what? Your mother was probably right! Humans are constantly competing with each other to see who is top dog. The only difference being that dogs usually show loyalty. I've spent years working this out.

The people who are mean, who gossip about you, who try to bring you down, are being ruled by an emotion they probably don't recognise and in many cases can't control. A while ago I came across another quote which really struck a chord with me. 'There are some people who always seem angry and continuously look for conflict. Walk away; the battle they are fighting isn't with you, it is with themselves.' I can't begin to tell you how true this is. I just wish I knew who originally said it. I'd send them flowers!

People who are constantly jealous come from a place of insecurity, fear and anxiety. They're driven by resentment and inadequacy and after many years of these emotions eating away at their soul, they wear themselves out and become bitter. As the philosopher Alain de Botton says, bitterness is anger that forgot where it came from.

Nasty people can also be scared and sad. They're the ones who are most urgently in need of compassion, not anger.

'If people are trying to bring you down, it only means that you are above them.' Unknown

For many years I worked with someone who didn't like me much (I know, I couldn't believe it either, who couldn't like me?!!!). We'd never really spoken and I couldn't work out why. Then I overheard them telling someone else that they thought I'd had an easy life and a blessed career path, that 'blondes with big tits' get everything in life.

What? That university degree followed by more than fifteen years of hard work in the media was an 'overnight success'? Working harder than many in the newsroom to prove that I was not a dumb blonde? (Although, as Dolly Parton once said, 'I know I'm not dumb, because I know I'm not blonde.') And having senior colleagues who could yell at you *and* stare down your top at the same time has just been a barrel of laughs … not!

Be choosy

When you think about it, you actually teach others how to treat you every day. Think about how you behave. Be selective about the parts of your life you share and with whom. There's absolutely nothing wrong with choosing what you tell people and who you let in. Not everyone needs to know every little thing about you.

We joke in my family that my mother is so open she would give strangers her credit card PIN. She wouldn't of course, but she is an over-sharer. Whether it's to please people or simply to fill silences my mum will give you all the information in her head, and then some more. Then she's surprised and in some cases upset when people use that information as gossip.

Unfortunately I have inherited this trait from my darling, open mum. It's one of the things I like least about myself. Having said all this, you might be wondering why I'm sharing a big part of my life and my innermost thoughts for all the world to read in this book! It's human nature to share – we've been doing it since the cavewoman days, sitting around the fire after we've collected the berries for dinner, bitching about how awful someone looks in her new mammoth-skin tunic.

Just be aware of what you're saying and what you're giving away about yourself. Keep part of you to yourself and those you trust most. Otherwise you're giving away some of your power and your peace.

Try not to complain too much about your lot in life – because that information will just fuel a nasty person's fire. Even if you think your life sucks, remember there are people out there worse off than you. If you don't want to be gossiped about, remember Her Majesty Queen Elizabeth's motto: 'Never complain. Never explain.'

Now I'm not encouraging you to be totally guarded and fake. That is an awful and sad way to live. Try to find a balance between being open and honest and keeping a part of yourself sacred.

Part of our job on *Sunrise* is to tell stories from our real lives. Many of these anecdotes are self-deprecating and embarrassing, some are hilarious; others are a little bit sad. As the only single

TOP: Meeting Tom Burlinson at the 2005 Logies.

LEFT: Charlie and I surprising Georgie on her 30th birthday in London, 2008.

TOP: Post DWTS 'cha-cha' with Mum and Dad.

BOTTOM: Farewelling Sky in Canberra to join Seven in Sydney (with David Speers and Tony Lynas).

LEFT: Meeting my idols Kath & Kim.

BELOW RIGHT: Editing our 6pm news package the day Schapelle Corby was sentenced — this is outside the courtroom on the street with cameraman Ben Emery.

BOTTOM: Loving my job while reporting on crocs in the NT.

RIGHT: A 'hot lap' for the V8s in Bathurst.

BELOW: Interviewing Brad Pitt on the red carpet.

TOP: Meeting Buzz Aldrin.

ABOVE LEFT: Covering the Queen's Diamond Jubilee for *Sunrise*.

ABOVE RIGHT: Fun with the *Sunrise* team at the Brownlows.

TOP: Riding a donkey in the Atlas Mountains, Morocco.

ABOVE: Travelling in Paris.

TOP: Holidaying In Rome.

ABOVE: Taking a cooking class with Mum in Tuscany.

ABOVE: Enjoying the crystal clear waters in Fiji.

LEFT: Georgie, Cinnamon and I.

member of the troupe, a lot of mine come from my single–dating life, which is often embarrassing, hilarious and a little bit sad.

I pride myself on being open and honest. Perhaps it's one of the reasons I got the job, but I always keep part of myself private, for my family, my close friends and my partner (if I have one!) away from the spotlight. Just for me.

Self Reflection

It's the old, original Sam. The one without all the make-up, the one with the freckles and curly hair. The ten-year-old who is obsessed with horses and Madonna. The thirteen-year-old who thinks her life is going to end when she gets braces and cries herself to sleep every night of her first term at boarding school. The sixteen-year-old who is boy-mad, even though the boys never look her way. The eighteen-year-old who panics in exams and doesn't do very well in the Higher School Certificate. The nineteen-year-old who has to sleep on the ground under the Eiffel Tower because she and her friends didn't know they'd have to book accommodation on Bastille Day. The 26-year-old who gets a job at a major TV network and doesn't know a thing about how to handle the office politics. The 32-year-old who still gets pimples. The 33-year-old who is sent to cover unrest in East Timor and has absolutely no idea where to start, but is too afraid to speak up. The 38-year-old who still (occasionally) argues with her mother, and STILL gets pimples.

All these moments shape us into the people we are now. Some are wonderful. Many are painful. Nobody knows exactly what we've been through, how that's shaped us, or what's going on in our heads right now – but that's what makes us all individuals.

The older I become, and the more clearly I look at my parents, I realise none of us really knows what we're doing on this earth. We're all just trying to work it out. So be kind to yourself and others.

Weigh up what's going on in your life and edit which bits people will be lucky enough to hear about. Even though people often complain about being busy, many of them actually don't have a lot going on in their lives, which leaves time for idle gossip and taking too much interest in other people's lives.

Gossip

It's important to be wary of gossip, both delivering it and receiving it. As Oscar Wilde once said, 'My own business always bores me to death, I prefer other people's.' No one got 'gossip' as well as Mr Wilde.

Try to let gossip wash over you and live your life well. Be aware when you say to someone, 'Don't tell anyone, but …', they will almost certainly tell many people, usually with exaggeration and/or a bit of hysteria thrown in. Sometimes if you want to communicate a message within your social circle or at work, it's okay. Sometimes

I consider this to be a kind of 'self-protecting-or-self-promoting-whatever-takes-your-fancy PR'.

A close girlfriend of mine works in a senior position in a male-dominated office in the city. She was going through numerous rounds of IVF trying to have a baby with her husband. It was a tough time and she was quite emotional at work. Although she had privately told her boss, she knew everybody would be talking. Rather than tell everyone in the office her most private details, she asked her PA to tell a few strategic people and soon enough the message was quietly out and it was no big deal and she was left alone.

I draw the line at leaking to the newspapers or publicly shaming people, which can be rife in my industry. Leaking to newspapers with the express purpose of bringing someone down is a despicable act and a slippery slope. I refuse to take part in it and have no respect or time for the people who do this. It usually comes back to bite them anyway – the identity of the leaker is inevitably revealed and no one ever trusts them again. In the end it's the leaker who is at the receiving end of the negative publicity. Being a sly and underhanded gossip does NOT protect you from nastiness in life.

Stick to your guns

One of my favourite expressions is, 'Keep your gun in your handbag'. In other words, don't go off at every little thing that bugs you, because nobody will listen to you when you're actually really pissed off about something. Be measured and your words will pack more punch.

People are always going to say and do things that irritate you and that you disagree with. At the school gate, the office, the gym, in your family – wherever there are humans there will be politics, and there will *always* be someone in your life who feels joy from seeing you unhappy.

You simply have to learn to let a lot of the stupidity and small-mindedness go – or you'll take it on as stress. Let it wash over you. If this comes naturally to you, then you're very lucky and you should get a medal! If you're more highly strung (like a lot of us) it can help to work out where the negativity is coming from.

It doesn't build you up to tear others down. Try to forgive, even if the other person is not sorry. It's best for your mental health – and takes away much of their power.

Remember, holding a grudge is letting someone live rent-free in your head. The best revenge is success. Stick to your guns and live your life.

Speak softly and carry a big stick

This is thought to be an African proverb advising caution and non-aggression in negotiation. Former US President Theodore Roosevelt brought it into the mainstream when he used it to refer to his foreign policy. This mentality can help us modern women quite nicely when dealing with negative people. Don't be a pushover, but don't let yourself sink to an unkind person's level. As the writer Paulo Coelho said, 'Don't allow your wounds to transform you into someone you are not.'

Here's another quote I love: 'Being nice to someone you'd rather slap isn't fake. It's sucking it up and acting like an adult.' Know when to fight for yourself. Like all things in life, it's about working out a balance. Confrontation is effective, but scary. Saying to someone who behaves negatively towards you, 'Is there a problem? Have I done something to offend you?' puts the ball back in their court.

Of course, true-blue bullies will run a mile from this sort of questioning. I once tried to reconcile with an unhappy work colleague, twice asking them to meet with me for coffee to sort out the reasons behind their behaviour towards me. Both times they didn't turn up.

If you're going to stick up for yourself, breathe deeply, know your argument and take ownership of your direction. Take responsibility for what you want. Be honest and be fair. Standing up for yourself in the correct way can give you clarity and certainty. You will be inspired and inspiring. You won't always win – but you should always try.

Embrace your femininity

The fashion designer Valentino says to all his models as he sends them down the runway, 'Be strong, be sophisticated, be feminine.' There's power to being feminine.

Think of some of the world's most powerful and assertive women: Angelina Jolie, Coco Chanel, Oprah Winfrey, Sheryl Sandberg, Beyoncé Knowles, Quentin Bryce, Mae West, Hillary Rodham Clinton, Melinda Gates, Janet Yellen, Fiona Wood, Gail Kelly, Ellen DeGeneres and Dora the Explorer (this is for my niece Lucia – who at the age of three believes Dora is the ultimate woman. Who knows – she could be right!).

Standing up for yourself might mean you need to call on your masculine energy and qualities. Pushing forward, confronting people, being rigid, using adrenaline to deal with nasty situations, these are all considered masculine traits. We are living in an increasingly 'masculine' and (from the Chinese symbol for masculine energy) '*yang*' society.

It's really important to try to balance this. Try to '*yin*' (the Chinese feminine) it up a bit. Your feminine side is about creation. If you feel burnt out, stressed, overworked and exhausted – you draw on your masculine energy to help you through and it's easy to lose touch with your feminine side. It happens to all of us.

Use your femininity, your softness, your nurturing side. Forgive people who have not done the right thing by you. Be smart. You can still be bold.

Make your life better; dance, write, paint, sing (any form of expression), play, dream, meditate on what changes you'd like to make, have a holiday, connect with the people you love, take a break from your smartphone, get back to nature – any or all of these things will restore your feminine energy, and then you'll be amazed by how your life will improve.

Bringing back your feminine side is essential for handling the dramas that crop up in life, especially those women create among themselves. Transforming your own life for the better will soothe and restore you, making you more resilient to cope with whatever life throws at you. Inspire yourself. Enliven yourself.

Enjoy being a woman. Help other women and rediscover your strength in your femininity.

Rising above it: in a nutshell

- Rising above it is the best way to deal with negativity.

- Let the other person be right occasionally; you don't always have to 'win'.

- Be happy for others.

- Walk away from conflict; tell your ego to 'cool it'.

- Live and let live.

- Do nice things for others and don't expect anything in return.

- Be flexible – with your relationships and your plans.

- Accept that people aren't perfect and they will do things that won't always please you.

- Think of criticism as 'commentary' and don't take it personally.

- Avoid over-sharing. Be selective about what parts of your life you share, and with whom.

- Find a balance; be open, but keep part of you sacred.

- Live in such a way that if someone speaks badly of you, no one will believe it.

- Ignore gossip.

- Try to forgive people, even if they are not sorry.

- Know when to fight for yourself – and when you do, have a plan.

- Embracing your feminine side will help you build resilience.

A woman of
substance

CHAPTER EIGHT

After I signed my second contract with Channel Seven I was finally earning some decent money, so I decided it was time to get serious and start acting like a grown-up. Until this point I had taken on the 'Bridget Jones' persona, hopeless with men and money – probably because I was both and it was better to embrace it than fight it. Whatever small amount of money I'd had in those days I'd spent on rent and clothes, so now that I had a bit extra, I asked around for advice and a colleague in the newsroom recommended a financial planning firm. I went to visit this place, and they must have seen me coming.

Single, (reasonably) high-earning female.

No idea.

The firm was entirely made up of men, and what little industry regulation there is today didn't really exist back then. While I did ask plenty of questions and I was cautious, I was also feeling financially ambitious: I wanted to own my own property, make investments and ensure I was paying the right amount of tax. I took their advice and followed their suggestions but in the end, every single 'product' and investment these blokes got me into probably only benefited them when they got their commissions and kickbacks.

The straw that broke the camel's back came one day, when I was quite rightly questioning some highly dubious decision and one of the planners leant over his desk, put his hand on mine, looked into my eyes and said, 'Don't you worry your pretty little head about it.'

Excuse me?

It's my money, and while I agree my head is pretty, piss off, mate. (Excuse my French.)

How patronising. How outrageous.

I left them the next day and took matters into my own hands. I changed banks and instantly found a cheaper interest rate and a better mortgage, bought and sold an investment property and my own apartment and discovered I was over-insured.

I'm still trying to sell one of the investments they acquired for me. I also missed out on the first home owner's grant because of these people. After all their bad advice, it's taken me a good many years to get myself set up, which I'm now proud to say, I am. In the past twelve months I've also had to deal with car salespeople and real estate agents, all men, and I'm sorry to say, their attitudes to women need to be greatly improved.

Believe it or not, when I decided that being 'a woman of substance' was going to be one of my 'Rules for Life', I wasn't actually thinking of the Barbara Taylor Bradford novel of the same name. Given I was just three years old when she wrote it in 1979, this is no real surprise, though. Somewhere along the way it must have entered my mind and that of millions of other women because this early-twentieth-century feminist rags-to-riches story sold more than 30 million copies and launched one of the most-watched TV mini-series of our time. The central theme of the book is the power of a woman, especially when she has relentless perseverance.

One of last century's bestselling popular fiction writers, 30 years later, when Barbara Taylor Bradford was asked about the novel *Fifty Shades of Grey*, she claimed it was 'not even sexy' … go, Babs!

It's a compliment to be called 'a woman of substance'. You don't know what life is going to throw at you, things won't always go your way, love never runs smoothly and your children, if you have them, will (mostly) not appreciate you fully.

These are all parts of life. As one of my favourite writers Alain de Botton says: 'You have to be bashed about by life a bit to see the point of daffodils, sunsets and uneventful "boring" days.'

Mostly life shows us that success comes from hard work. This chapter is about being a *wo*man of substance. It doesn't matter what era you live in.

Tips for being a woman of substance

Be happy with who you are

Work out who you are, how you got there and where you want to go. Make peace with yourself, because you're stuck with you your whole life, so you'd better learn to love, or at least really, really like, yourself.

> *Embrace your individuality: it's what makes you stand out from the crowd.*

Find your voice

When I was a child, if an adult spoke to me I would blush bright red up my neck and all over my face. I was so shy, it was ridiculous. Then gradually I became more and more confident until I was a fully fledged teenage smart-arse. As an adult I've calmed down and found true quiet confidence. I've also found my voice. If you watch

Sunrise, you'll notice I really *have* found my voice. I'm not backward in putting myself out there. Your voice doesn't have to be loud. In fact it can pack more punch sometimes when it's quiet.

But use it. That's why God/Buddha/Mohammed gave it to you.

Work out what your dream is, then make it happen

Everybody starts somewhere. I was once that terrified little work experience kid reading newspapers in the corner of a newsroom. Persevere and be tough. Work hard, turn up, listen to people who know more than you and learn from them. Take risks (within reason).

Live your values

Trust your instincts. Don't sign anything you're not sure of. Don't deal with anyone you're not sure of. Ask questions. Be honest, but be firm. Be true to yourself.

Set standards

Be discerning. Set standards in everything from relationships, to work, clothing, linen and books. You may not believe this, but I've made many bad decisions and stayed in relationships way too long because I've ignored my gut instinct. If you're like me, your gut is loud and discriminating, yet time and time again, I've pushed mine down and told it to shut up.

Those days are gone for me. I try to *feel*, not just *think*, listening to my instincts and emotions more deeply, not just the immediate thoughts in my mind. This is one of the major things we women can do to help ourselves set the right standards for ourselves. We have been wired with this unbelievable in-built radar to detect danger and dangerous people (I don't mean bank robbers, I mean emotionally destructive people). All I can say is, please listen to it.

There's the misguided notion that being in love means life is complete, that a romantic relationship is the end to all life's problems. A man is not the answer, and staying with the wrong man just to avoid being lonely will create all sorts of headaches.

Work on yourself to ensure *you* are the person who makes your own life complete. Then you'll be ready to enter into a loving, healthy relationship.

Reconsider any relationships you have that might be toxic. Set your standards high, you deserve it; never let people treat you like dirt, and stand up for yourself if you're being treated unfairly.

Call on your values at work, and stick to them. Your boss will respect you for having standards because it shows you care about your work. Every employer is looking for a self-respecting employee.

Set standards for how you treat other people and stick to them.

Be strong, respectful and polite and you will reap the rewards.

Set standards for your physical appearance. Make sure your clothes show the world who you are. As a girlfriend of mine said to me after her second baby, when she was home in a cloud of vomit and nappies, 'If you dress tracksuit pants, you feel tracksuits pants.' Nice clothes don't have to be expensive; just let them reflect who you are and what you want to say.

Throw out anything – clothing, linen, napkins, tea towels – with holes in it, except those expensive jeans that already have holes in them. My dad finds this so hilarious.

Take care of your home and look after your possessions. It probably took hard work to obtain them, so respecting them will mean you respect yourself.

Use your good china. Use your favourite linen. Why else do you have them? You deserve to use them right now. Stop waiting for a 'special occasion', you could get hit by a bus tomorrow.

Never stop taking chances

Put yourself in positions where you might fail. When the Channel Seven bosses offered me the hosting position on *Sunrise* in 2013, it was a big gamble. They knew it, and I knew it. There would be a lot of attention, and I was warned I may have to toughen up a bit. I did, and it turned out to be a wonderful and successful transition.

I've learned so much about myself as a woman and how much I can handle.

Every time I speak to a room full of people, I become extremely nervous. Stick me in front of a camera with a million people watching and I don't bat an eyelid. Put me in front of a room full of sixteen-year-old schoolgirls and my hands start to sweat.

I really pushed my limits with *Dancing with the Stars*. I am not a dancer, but I'm proud that I gave it a red-hot go. It was not easy, or even particularly fun if I'm honest. The rewards were great, though, especially on a personal level. It was a fantastic experience, I met some wonderful people and I even learned to dance, a little bit. But the main thing was I faced my fears and I didn't flinch.

When I put myself out there, whether it's on national TV or in a school hall, I could look like a complete failure and a laughing stock and if I stuff up, there is no hiding it. I chose to take each of these experiences and let them help me grow as a woman. I'm proud to have been brave.

Now I can say with all conviction, this is not my first rodeo.

You have to make a choice to take a chance, or your life will never change.

My motto is, bite off more than you can chew, and then chew like buggery!

Be brave

One of the loveliest things someone has ever said to me was in the newsroom, which is surprising, given it's often not a particularly cheerful place. I was being badly battered in one newspaper after taking over the *Sunrise* hosting role. Peter Meakin, my former news director, a mentor and the man responsible for my employment at Channel Seven, took me into his office and said to me, 'Sam, one of things I like most about you is that you are brave. You need to hold your line.'

I had always considered myself to be brave and had always tried to privately live my life that way. I was upset because it was a pretty awful time. It should have been joyful. I hadn't done anything wrong except get a promotion.

So I will be forever thankful that someone acknowledged that, and said it out loud. It gave me renewed energy and confidence to continue to hold my head up. To 'hold my line'.

Sometimes you just need to be brave living your everyday life, like when you're buying a house or a car. Or it might be something on a bigger scale, a career or family issue.

Now when I say 'brave', I don't mean stupid brave. Never test the depth of the water with both feet. I make sure I think things through and absolutely *never* react in anger. At the same time, I do choose when to stand up for myself. And I might feel like taking revenge but I actually feel better if I write down my revenge plan on a piece of paper, then burn it. Karma can be a bitch so you want yours to be good.

Voodoo is also excellent …

Be honest

When I was a young cadet reporter in Canberra I made a mistake one day. I was 22 and felt the responsibility of my job. I can't remember what I actually did, but I remember that I was guilty and the news director berated me for it in front of the whole newsroom. How embarrassing. I owned it and apologised.

Later, another colleague tracked me down privately and said, 'If you want to get ahead, don't ever admit anything is your fault again.' Television is a tough world. I was shocked and confused. It was probably the first time my values had really been rocked and it was a massive, disappointing insight into the industry I had chosen.

I'm happy to say after many years, I still always try to own my mistakes and never blame others for them. I do, however, have a little problem with tact. It's an Armytage thing. We're all like it, we just blurt out whatever's in our heads. Like when I interviewed film director JJ Abrams I told him that I loathed science fiction. Problem was, I was reviewing his new blockbuster, *Star Trek*. He looked a little shocked. I prefer to think he might have been proud of me. Actually I'm sure he never thought twice about it. We were both baffled as to why the office had sent me on that assignment.

Sometimes my 'honesty' can be hurtful and I'm very aware of that. It's something I work on every day. Although I still really hate sci-fi.

Working hard

If you want to be taken seriously, show up on time, be prepared and do the work. No one is an overnight success. Believe it or not, even many reality TV stars have usually been hovering around with an agent waiting to pounce onto our screens. I don't know one single person who has achieved success in their lives without hard work. I have spent many, many years on late shift and breakfast shift – sometimes both in one day! Under the enormous pressure of live TV and deadlines, I've written stories on breaking news sitting in a gutter outside a Balinese courthouse. I've worked in freezing conditions, boiling conditions, been spat on and had my hair stuck down by gaffer tape by a cameraman in a windstorm, all in the name of gathering news. I've worked Christmas Day, Easter, public holidays and been called back to work from many of my overseas breaks.

I'm starting to sound like a martyr now, but you get the message. If you want to make it, it takes hard work and not always in airconditioning or between nine and five.

Do your fair share of the work but don't forget to speak up for yourself. Please don't suffer in silence. Believe it or not, I used to do that. As I mentioned above, I've found my voice (and it's loud) but this has only come with age and confidence. It's vitally important we women find our voices in the workplace.

Recognise what's a fair workload and when you're being used. If it's ridiculous and unfair and you've worked hard, then politely say you've done your share and leave the office. If you don't draw the line, you'll inevitably get sick, or come a cropper in some other way. The first responsibility you have is to yourself. Work–life balance is crucial.

Women, particularly single women, often shoulder more than their fair share of the load because we're terrible at saying no. Men are excellent at setting boundaries and mothers often have a good reason to leave the office, but single girls are big targets in the extra workload department.

I love Sheryl Sandberg's book *Lean In*. She tells a story of how, about six months after she started at Facebook, Mark Zuckerberg sat her down for her first review. He told her that her desire to be liked by everyone would hold her back. He said that when you want to change things, you can't please everyone. If you do please everyone, you aren't making enough progress.

I, too, am a people pleaser. It's in my nature to be obedient. I was raised in the 'children are to be seen and not heard' generation. In the past I have gone against my values and even my instincts and put my mental and physical health and safety in jeopardy for my career. It's human nature to want everyone to like you, but be prepared to rock the boat a little. Otherwise you won't get anything of value done.

Seek out people of great intellect (maybe even smarter than you are!). Besides making you look better, you can also be inspired by them. There's an old expression, 'Hire people who are smarter than you, then get out of their way.'

My boss at *Sunrise* is a 31-year-old gay man. Although we cater for everyone, our main demographic for the show is middle-aged women, and although he has sound judgment on what makes a good TV show, my boss has surrounded himself with producers from all walks of life. One is a mother of four in her forties. Another is a quiet, conservative family man. Then there are a few young girls in their twenties who are excellent young women but they also want to have a bit of fun. It's a great balance. There's always someone in there to test out ideas on. And most importantly, people who can say, 'No, that won't appeal to my age group.'

Listen to others and recognise experience when you see it. As my father says, 'You aren't learning much if your lips are moving.'

I don't mind admitting I'm a total control freak. I have a dogged belief that I'm usually right and nobody can do things as well as I can, but one of the major things I've learned as I've matured (yeah right!) is to recognise when to let go and bow to the people who know more than me about certain subjects.

Tweak things. Work them through and partner with people who you trust and respect. Respect is hugely important. I would find it almost impossible to work for anyone I didn't respect.

Mentoring

Seek out mentors. If you're lucky, these people will come to you naturally in your life – and they can be both men and women. I have a few mentors of both genders whom I admire greatly. Some have been bosses, but a few are just cool, older women in my private life. I find my mentors *invaluable* when times are tough or there are big decisions to be made. They have given me advice on how to deal with men in the workplace, how to deal with women in the workplace (far more difficult), how to deal with the press, managing my brand, what jobs to take and what jobs not to take, along with invaluable insights when I'm dating.

More and more women are seeking out mentors these days, which is terrific. Think of mentoring as the modern girl enlisting a guide. It's a jungle out there, and you can't navigate it on your own. It's also invaluable for older women in the workforce who might sometimes feel a little invisible, to have the next generation looking to them for help.

If you're like me, your major female role model, your mum, can't really help you with issues like office politics. She'll listen till the cows come home, bless her, but she's never worked in an office and she's certainly never worked in a newsroom, so naturally she doesn't really know what I'm going through at work.

Some of my work-related mentors have come my way by accident, which is kind of a nice, organic way for it to happen. The key to finding a mentor at work is to find someone you respect; you know you'll listen to them. Don't ask anybody and everybody for advice, you'll just confuse yourself. And I'll let you in on a little secret, a lot of people you work with don't actually know as much as you think they do. There are a lot of bluffers out there.

Look for people who have actually been through what you're going through. I have gravitated towards former news directors, older women who've retired from the media, and some who still work in it, and an aunt who remained single and had a career by choice, which is not common in my country family!

These people will be different from your girlfriends, mainly because they're likely to be more industry related, and they won't (or shouldn't) sugar-coat things. They should be totally honest with you, even if it's something you don't want to hear. Your girlfriends won't always be like that because they don't want to hurt you, bless them.

That's okay, you gain different things you need from different people in this life.

Be in control of your finances

Do not leave this up to a man, and never expect a man to be the solution to all your cashflow problems. Almost half of Australian households now have a female breadwinner, so it's time to stop playing it ditzy. Know where your money is AT ALL TIMES.

- Never sign anything you don't understand
- Have a debit card or a credit card with a reasonably low limit, say $1000, for your everyday living and to make purchases on the internet. (Be VERY AWARE of credit card and identity fraud, it's terrifying and can happen to any of us.) By all means own more than one credit card, just be strict about paying

it off. Credit card fees are as much dead money as parking tickets. Don't give your bank any more money than you have to and don't be talked into a higher limit than you need: have it high enough that you can help yourself in an emergency, but low enough that it doesn't tempt you to buy things you don't need or, more importantly, can't afford.

- Save as much as you can afford. I pay my salary into a savings account then pay myself a living allowance. This sounds strict, however I can still access my money if I need to buy something special (I treat myself often ... I work hard, right?) but it means I have forced savings and I have to think twice before I blow my cash. I have bought SO many things I don't use ... exercise bike, anyone?

- Work out a budget and try to stick to it – no excuses! Every year I set a budget for all my bills and commitments, plus a spending allowance, then I keep an eye on it each month to see if I'm on track.

- Shop around for the best offers and deals. Don't feel guilty about telling banks, insurance companies, energy providers, phone companies and real estate agents that you will go elsewhere if they can't improve their offers. You'll be amazed how often they miraculously become cheaper and work harder for you.

Buying property

It could be a long-term dream, or you might be financially ready to jump into the property market right now. Whatever position you're in, buying your own home can be a worthwhile investment. If you work out the sums, you could be paying your own mortgage with what you're paying in rent to your landlord. As we all know, though, Australian property prices are among the highest in the world so if you are interested in buying property, keep an eye on the market and seek out good advice. Read books, talk to people, hear their stories, but try not to listen to too many people. It's like face products and everything else in life, everyone has something you should try. Do your research, know what you want and hold your line.

A few years ago, I took the plunge and bought a tiny apartment. I made it look gorgeous with plantation shutters, white paint and floorboards and it was a much-loved first home. I was able to sell it easily when I decided I needed a slightly bigger place.

You need to know what you're doing when you apply for a mortgage. Why don't they teach this stuff in schools? So much handier than algebra …You need to be aware of mortgage insurance, how much you really need for a deposit and to understand stamp duty.

If you own your own home, paying your mortgage off should be your number-one financial priority. Put any excess money, bonuses, tax refunds, Lotto winnings (haha) into your mortgage. See if your bank offers an offset account. Rather than having spare funds in a taxable bank account, putting it against your mortgage will speed up your repayments and will reduce your tax bill.

Investing

Diversify your savings into one or more investments. Have some shares, some cash and consider income protection insurance, or six months' wages in the bank, in case you fall ill or are injured. I know that sounds negative, but it's sensible and with a bit of budgeting it's doable.

I'm an old-fashioned bricks-and-mortar investor, so I have stepped into the investment property market. I'm able to negatively gear my mortgage repayments, which reduces my tax bill, and I'm hoping the value of the property will increase over time.

If you're looking into buying an investment property, as above, seek advice and know the market. If you're selling a property, know how to negotiate on a real estate agent's commission and be brave and self-assured all the way through. Don't put up with complacency; plenty of agents will coast because they're lazy (the property market is so hot, they can afford to be!) and they think that when they're dealing with a woman they can slack off. Many will negotiate with you on their commission, and then you should make them work for it.

If you make a capital gain on an investment property, you could be paying up to 50 per cent capital gains tax, so check everything before you jump in. Ultimately, if this is not your industry, you don't know much about finance (me) and your father was a farmer, so you weren't taught about finance (me), you need to ask the right experts. I can't emphasise enough to talk to people in the know and ask for help.

When I bought my tiny apartment I was seriously mucked around by one of the big banks. They were really playing hardball and while I was completely frustrated I didn't know how to play back. I'd interviewed Aussie Home Loans' John Symond many times on *Sunrise* and chatted to him at the races. He's a very nice man, and he knows a thing or two about mortgages! At the suggestion of my boyfriend at the time, I emailed Aussie John's personal assistant asking politely for some direction, and John himself wrote straight back with the name of his personal mortgage broker, who was fantastic and has been part of my financial life ever since. Now I'm not suggesting you all hit up Aussie John, but always make sure you find someone trustworthy for advice.

Do not watch the Kardashians

You will not learn anything of substance from the Kardashians. A woman of substance does not watch this shallow, banal rubbish. She has better things to do with her time. Read a book, go for a walk, ring a friend – the list is endless.

Do not confuse yourself with any of them, mainly because you haven't sold your life rights (ergo, your soul) for notoriety to a group of wealthy producers sitting in LA.

But who am I to complain about reality TV? You can't argue with popularity – well you could but you'd be wrong. My GP once told me that if you're desperate to get a doctor's appointment you should book between 4.30pm and 5pm because that's when *The Bold and the Beautiful* is on and people are glued to their sets at home. Unbelievable, but true.

Ever since the OJ Simpson trial people have been falling over their couches to watch has-beens or wannabes living out their lives on television. In case you don't know, these 'fly-on-the-wall' shows are scripted. The people on them are mostly contrived characters with no discernible skills or talent, and they are adding little to our society. These people are recognised, but they are not to be admired.

I understand the need for mindless entertainment as relaxation in our busy society, but try programs like *The Simpsons*. After I've been covering breaking news and my brain needs a rest from all the death and despair, this is my go-to show. It's well written and clever, and entertaining and relaxing.

Fame is *not* the be-all and end-all. Fame is actually quite over-rated … just ask any Hollywood A-lister (*not* the D-listers in reality TV), who are tirelessly pursued by paparazzi, and whose lives are no longer their own. Fame is rarely forever, and then you're just left with … you. I really worry about this next generation of kids who live their life on social media. Fame seems to be their only real goal.

I'd like to think that if my life on TV disappeared tomorrow, and it easily could, that I would have other skills, other things that made me interesting, made me money and kept me interested. I'm constantly seeking ways to learn new skills (like writing this book!).

Your stars and the supernatural

It might be fun for a bit of a laugh, but try not to read your stars too often. If you do, do not take them too seriously: do not make major life decisions based on them. I know I'm unhappy when I start reading my stars. Read the other star signs on the page – they could ALL be you! Again, do something better with your time – a book?

I might not be the biggest fan of astrology, but I have to admit I have visited several clairvoyants, although I've always left feeling more confused than when I arrived. I like to be open to the universe, but I'm also aware that our minds have an enormous ability to make things happen.

Years ago I bought a little weekender cottage on a couple of acres in the country. I sold it when my accountant told me I was way too young to have a weekender and that I should get myself to a nightclub and stop being a nanna ... Anyway, it was a gorgeous little miner's cottage from about the 1840s, and it was haunted.

I did it up and made it look really cute, but it didn't seem to love me back. It kept hurting me – windows would suddenly fall down on my hands (I broke three fingers!); paintings would fall off walls; a lightbulb once ended up on the floor beside the bedside table; and the hot tap in the shower would get stuck and scald me. Maybe it was just an old house, but I thought it was like spending my weekends in the place from *Poltergeist*. Not relaxing.

I asked the priest from the local village's Catholic church to come and bless it, or exorcise it, or whatever ... and bless him, he played along. He waved a bit of holy water about, I gave him a cup of tea and the house felt more calm after that. Placebo effect? Highly likely, but whatever works, I say. I don't mind ghosts, but they have to be friendly.

Watch your attitude

It's been said countless times, but you only get one life, so you might as well enjoy it. If you take yourself too seriously, you'll miss out on a lot of what life has to offer. Plus, taking yourself too seriously can be bor-ing!

Believe in something, whether it be charity, politics, religion, sport (some in Australia might say these last two are one and the same). Try not to be a victim. Try not to be a martyr. If you don't like your life, change it.

'One must dare to be happy.' Gertrude Stein

Imagine the person everyone wants to chat to at a party. What is it about these people that makes them so attractive? Usually they're relaxed in their own skin, optimistic, fun and interesting. Be that person.

Pretend your life is a movie (see Chapter Ten, 'Be the Leading Lady in the Movie of Your Life') and take centre stage. Give them the old razzle-dazzle …

You don't have to be sugary nice. Hell, I'm the girl who wanted the marines to win in the movie *Avatar*. Have a backbone, stand up for what you believe in and treat people as you would like to be treated. Be kind. Don't gossip, stay out of office politics and think good thoughts.

Gambling with the important things

I know I've advocated taking risks in these pages, but not when it comes to gambling. I don't recommend it. I'm not talking about a few harmless dollars (even $50!) on Melbourne Cup

Day. Maybe another $50 on Derby Day, or even a few bucks on Number 7 in the 7th at the Wagga Gold Cup. It would be un-Australian not to.

Don't gamble with your finances, your life, your reputation, your health. Don't waste your hard-earned cash on:

- Cigarettes
- Poker machines
- Any piece of exercise machinery you see advertised on TV that will end up collecting dust in your spare room – you will not get abs like the professionals in three easy payments.

Remember, in most gambling scenarios, the house always wins. Have fun, but always remember the quickest way to double your money is to fold it in half and put it back in your pocket.

- If you find yourself in a compromising situation, get yourself out of there and to somewhere safe
- Never ever, ever sit on the floor of a public toilet – unless you're seriously sick – if you're just drunk, go home!
- Don't spread gossip
- Don't believe everything you read in the newspapers and believe very little of what you read in women's magazines

- If you lie down with dogs you'll get up with fleas
- Don't rip people off
- If something sounds too good to be true, it probably is
- Don't post too much of your life on Facebook or Instagram – enjoy your life privately
- Don't give out your personal details over the phone or internet
- Don't talk up your abilities – let your achievements do the talking.

Giving back

Try to be a good human. Find a charity or a cause you believe in and give back in any small way you can. We can sometimes experience donor fatigue, but we must constantly remind ourselves how lucky we are in this country. You only have to go overseas to realise that.

You don't have to be Bill Gates to make a difference. Donate your time if you cannot afford to give money. Ronald McDonald House (my charity during *Dancing with the Stars*) does amazing work for regional families with sick kids and they're always looking for helpers. Do you know how bored those kids are all day, stuck in hospital? Go and read a book to some of them ... It'll take a few hours out of your day, and brighten theirs. And their parents will get a few hours off to go and buy a paper and have a coffee.

You can make a difference and you know the best bit? It'll make you feel better about yourself. If you're feeling down and depressed, the easiest way to lift your mood is to help someone else.

I'm an ambassador for a few charities. I try not to spread myself too thin because I want to give them as much energy as I can and get behind the things I really believe in. One is the Sony Foundation, the philanthropic arm of Sony Music, so they really have the power to make things happen. The Foundation does some wonderful work for teenagers with cancer.

Helping in the community, in no matter how small a way, is one of the best things you can do for your soul.

The other foundation close to my heart is Soldier On, a fantastic organisation that helps rehabilitate our physically and psychologically wounded soldiers. With men on both sides of my family going away to war, this cause is something I deeply believe in. So many of our young men and women returning from Afghanistan and Iraq are suffering from post-traumatic stress disorder. Soldier On was set up by a young soldier, John Bale, whose mate died in action in Afghanistan and he vowed to do more to help the people who serve our nation. It's supported by Prime Minister Tony Abbott, several former prime ministers and the Governor-General, Sir Peter Cosgrove. The patron is Victoria Cross recipient and national hero Mark Donaldson.

Both charities are very rewarding … and I'm honoured to be able to help out wherever I can.

Through *Sunrise* we are approached for help by so many Australians in difficulty. I'm proud to say we do as much as we can to help them all. It's a privileged position to have the power to change people's lives and I look forward to being able to help those less fortunate for many years to come.

My 'how-to' guide for modern life
How to take a good photo
I know Instagram filters can make anyone look like Gisele, but to take a flattering photo that doesn't need a filter, angle your chin down, not to a ridiculous point, but so that you have a jawline. Never ever, ever say 'cheese' or anything else people tell you to say in photos. It's the worst thing for your face to be doing. Angle your body so it has some shape, try moving your arm away slightly to show your waist. Never stand straight on – angle your body slightly. Bend one knee so your hips and thighs look slimmer.

How to make friends as an adult

Find people who have common interests. Ask them lots of questions. Trust is built up over time, so be a little cautious. I know this is true at work. Shared experiences make for friendships. You'll also meet great new people at places where you have shared interests. I've been to a health retreat twice in the past three years for holidays, and both times I've met fantastic, like-minded girls who will be lifelong friends.

How to deal with haters on social media

Block, block, block. That is all.

How to write a book – (with difficulty!)

Writing a book is tough and time consuming – why did I agree to it *this year*??? Write what you know. Find a publisher (who's lovely, like mine) and sit down in front of your laptop. I find it easier to write in two-hour blocks. Then I get up and go for a walk. I like writing in a café – I like the noise – if I'm at home the TV/fridge are toooooo tempting!

How to bluff your way through security

It's an oldie but a goodie: act like you're meant to be there and you don't have time to deal with security guards, even though you're privately terrified of them. When I covered Michael Jackson's funeral, security was super tight, even for the media. I didn't have the kind of media ID they were asking for, but believe it or not, I got through that wall of LA policemen brandishing a piece of plastic that had been handed to me in the boardroom at Channel Seven – it was for completing a quick course on bushfires.

How to cope when your younger sister gets married before you

This happened to me obviously, and I have to admit it wasn't easy. Of course I was so happy for her, but I was going through a break-up at the time that made it tough. Luckily we like the bloke she married, so *that* made it easier. Sometimes you just have to plaster on a smile and do your crying in private. (I find the car and the shower are the best places for this.) When I did Georgie's hair and make-up for her big day, I had no idea what I was doing and she didn't care because she works in banking and isn't vain like me, so everyone was a winner.

How to fix something electrical when it stops working

1. Turn it off and on again at the power point.
2. If this doesn't work, call an expert.

How to be normal

As Alain de Botton says, 'The only people we think of as normal are those we don't know yet.' Nobody is normal. We all have dysfunctional families. We all have moments of insecurity. We're all just doing our best in the world. Be happy with what you have and make it work.

How to avoid turning into your mother

I'm sorry but this is inevitable. It's also a positive thing. Look for the good in your mum-traits and work on what you don't like so much. I'm also starting to turn into my dad. I looked at a $450 pair of torn jeans in a shop the other day and thought, who would pay that much money for jeans with holes in them?! I might start growing ear hair and drenching cattle any minute now ...

a woman of substance: in a nutshell

- You are powerful.

- Persevere; nothing worth anything comes easily.

- Hard work equals success.

- Be happy with who you are.

- Find your voice.

- Work out what your dream is, then make it happen.

- Live your values.

- Set standards throughout your life.

- Be in control of your finances at all times.

- Never sign anything you don't understand.

- Save as much as you can afford.

- Work out your budget and stick to it!

- Do not confuse yourself with anyone from the Kardashians.

- Be multi-skilled.

- Don't read your stars.

- If you take your life too seriously, it ceases to be funny.

- Don't gamble with your money, your life, your reputation or your health.

- Give back – find something you believe in and help out.

- Seek out mentors to help you navigate through life.

Family is
fundamental

CHAPTER NINE

$\mathcal{I}$n 2011, as I mentioned in Chapter Two, I agreed to appear as a contestant on Dancing with the Stars (DWTS). The producers had asked me to do it the year before, but I wasn't quite ready. I had a quiet confidence even though I'd never danced before (and I mean NEVER), but I was reasonably fit and could usually pick up any sport I turned my hands or legs to. Well, it turned out I couldn't pick up dancing. I was dreadful.

The worst bit wasn't even remembering the highly complicated routines, or my cousin's four-year-old asking, 'Why is Sammy dancing with a lady?'... it was the acting component. I'm not overly graceful and I just couldn't bring myself to do all the over-the-top arm movements that are part-and-parcel of this style of dancing. And it was dancing on television, so it needed to be even more exaggerated. People were stopping me in the street saying how sorry *they felt for me, telling me how 'brave' I was. I begged them to stop voting for me.*

Mum and Dad, bless them, came to every show. Bearing in mind they witnessed three of my hockey games in all my years of boarding school in Sydney, this was quite a feat. It was a ten-hour round trip from their place to Melbourne, where DWTS was being filmed.

*Each week I was crucified. It was car-crash TV. Perfect for the producers, not so wonderful for my poor little soul. As the weeks progressed, Mum warned me, 'Your father is getting angrier, I think he's going to punch Todd McKenney!'** My father is not a violent man, but he is six foot two, a farmer and extremely protective of his firstborn. Friends and family are put in the best seats in the house, to the right of the judges, so I went to the producers and requested that Mum and Dad be moved a little further away to avoid putting the 'real' in reality TV. When the chips are down and you're being publicly humiliated in front of the nation, a girl's dad is about the most loyal person on the planet.*

** Dad would never have actually punched Todd McKenney. He just felt like it. FYI I love Todd and have totally forgiven him for any 'criticisms'.

Also FYI – I came fourth!!!!!!!!!!!!!!

When my profile first began to rise and people began asking about my childhood, I was surprised by their reaction. Journalists used the phrase 'idyllic country childhood' when they mentioned me. I had never thought of it as being terribly special. In fact, I thought it was very normal and at times very dull.

I am proud of where I grew up and had a wonderful upbringing, but Adaminaby, a quiet little town of about 250 people, wasn't particularly sophisticated. Dad managed a pastoral company for a Greek ship owner based in Athens, so the property we grew up on, Bolaro Station, was not 'ours', but we knew and loved every inch of it.

When I was six, *Phar Lap* was filmed at the racetrack on the property. It was meant to be Agua Caliente, Tijuana, Mexico in 1932; instead it was 51 years later at the height of the Adaminaby drought. Mum was an extra – you can pick her clapping in the grandstand, sitting behind Judy Davis. I was obsessed with horses and movies about horses for my entire childhood. The best bit, and the highlight of my life to that point, was that I got to meet Tom Burlinson, star of the movie *The Man from Snowy River*, who I was absolutely in love with. I see him now at the Logies and remind him, much to his amusement.

Local legend has it that Banjo Paterson, who would often come down from Sydney and stay at Bolaro in the 1880s, had written

'The Man From Snowy River' about a stockman who worked on the property, Charlie McKeahnie. Charlie had been killed while mustering, falling off his horse and breaking his neck. Although the Murrumbidgee River, not the Snowy River, runs through Bolaro, I believe in my heart that this beautiful mountain property inspired Mr Paterson.

Novelist Patrick White worked as a jackaroo on Bolaro in the early 1930s and his first novel, *Happy Valley*, was inspired by his time working near Adaminaby. The book was awarded the Australian Literature Society's gold medal in 1941.

At Adaminaby Public School we learned about the Snowy-Hydro scheme, and each summer we'd water-ski on one of its creations, Lake Eucumbene. We also learned about the Kiandra gold rush and would drive through the historic settlement every weekend on our way to the ski fields.

In 1992, US Defense Secretary (and later Vice President) Dick Cheney was in Canberra meeting with then-Prime Minister Paul Keating, following commemorations for the 50th anniversary of the Battle of the Coral Sea. Dad's boss had built a relationship with the US government. During a meeting in Washington before his visit to Australia, Mr Cheney had mentioned how much he loved fly-fishing. Adaminaby, and to be more precise, Bolaro, is the best place in Australia for brown and rainbow trout (in 1999 we hosted the World Fly Fishing Championships on the property). So it was organised that Dick Cheney, one of the most powerful men in the world, would swing by.

He arrived in a huge helicopter with his daughter and security team and fished in the river. We gave them a barbecue lunch, lamb from the property on the spit, followed by pavlova, and my brother, Charlie, had a ride in a helicopter with Cheney's security detail. Dick's daughter fell in the river that day and Mum lent her my tracksuit pants to get home. She never returned them. Let's just let that one go, shall we.

At least no one got shot.

The older I get, the more I appreciate my family. Like everything else when you're young, you don't appreciate what you have. I insisted on a masking-tape strip dividing the bedroom I shared with my younger sister, Georgie, as a child. We even had a strip down the wardrobe. She and I shared a bath as little girls and Mum would put me up the tap end, as I was the responsible one: I wouldn't turn on the 'hot' and scald us both. She'd leave us to play and when she came back, Georgie would be lying sprawled over the length of the bath, hands behind her head. I was pushed sideways, knees under my chin, quietly waiting for Mum to release me. We have an expression in our house that 'Sam grew up under the taps'. I want you to know, I am two years older than her.

When I was eight and Georgie was six, Charlie came along. I adored my new baby brother and loved changing his nappy, one time putting the pin through his skin (he didn't cry!). I used to carry him around as if he were mine. As he grew older, though, he became more annoying, trying to join our playtime and integrate his GI Joe doll into our Barbie games and hanging around when I had friends staying for slumber parties. Georgie and I told him he was adopted and that we found him at McDonald's. Once we even tied him to the clothesline with a skipping rope and put the sprinkler on him.

We have apologised to him profusely. Needless to say, though, he has never let us forget. He has grown up to be a wonderful young man and now has a family of his own.

Despite the fact Georgie and I sound like serial torturers, we all had wonderful, happy, simple and fun-filled childhoods. As young girls, Georgie and I adored playing tea parties in the garden with Mum. We learned the art of play, making pirate ships out of the willow trees along the banks of the Murrumbidgee River. Dad made us a billy cart and we would hook it to the back of the four-wheel motorbike. We played 'shops' under the pine trees and put soapy water over the trampoline, then jumped off a ladder onto it. All of it was unsupervised and free, well, except for the fuel for the motorbike – thanks, Dad!

It was tough at times but we were well loved. We weren't praised much, in fact we were left to our own devices much of the time. No fuss was made about our appearances; we did not strive to be beautiful or skinny. We were encouraged to be self-sufficient, smart and well read. My parents believed children were to be 'seen and not heard', although we were generally encouraged to speak to adults and take part in their conversations when we were with them.

We lived outdoors and were tough, strong and healthy. If you fell off your horse, you had to get straight back on. If you were thirsty, you drank water (sometimes out of the tap). If you didn't think you were capable of something Dad would say, 'Don't die wondering.' In our house there was no such word as 'can't'.

We were not wealthy or sophisticated. I was one of the youngest of a large tribe of Catholic cousins to go through my boarding school, and we only ever wore hand-me-down uniforms and shoes. Luckily for Mum and Dad it was cool to have a faded tunic and beaten-up brown Clarks ... so this was the ideal situation for all of us.

We didn't go on overseas holidays, in fact we barely went on holidays at all. For a few years we spent a couple of weeks in Surfers Paradise, which was a three-day drive from Adaminaby in our old green Commodore station wagon (it had about two million kilometres on the odometer by the time we finally sold it). Dad would smoke cigarettes and listen to the cricket on the radio as he drove. He possessed a great ability to listen to AM radio stations even when they were not tuned in properly and since a fair chunk of the drive up the eastern seaboard was through regional areas with weak signals, we mostly listened to static. I'm sure it was the same for everyone in those days ...?

This was an era BAC (before airconditioning), so Georgie, Charlie and I would fight for territory on that boiling plastic back seat for the best part of three days. I was also car sick all the way. This is why we probably preferred staying at home.

At Adaminaby Public School, there were two dozen kids in two classrooms. In year six, I was one of just six students. As I mentioned earlier in these pages, I was sent to boarding school in Sydney when I was thirteen. In my year there were 76 girls. I'd never even been to a McDonald's before. I missed my horse. I missed our dogs. I even missed Georgie and Charlie. I longed for Mum and Dad and the sound of cattle grazing in the paddock outside my window at home. I cried myself to sleep every night for a term.

Parents, they do the best they can

The majority of parents do the best job they know how. When you're little you think your parents know everything. As you grow older it slowly dawns on you that they are just doing their best.

They are only human. I've come to recognise that they are scarred and scared and moulded by experiences and hurts, just as we all are. They don't always know what they're doing and often they're lacking in confidence. I'm no longer young enough to think I know everything and find myself relying more and more heavily on my parents for their cool, calm heads and experience in life.

Try not to be too hard on your oldies and try not to blame them for all your faults, although I do blame my mother for my hair ... I look at who I have become and know that what I have made of myself is due in part to my parents. I'm grateful and proud.

Heritage

Embrace your heritage and family traditions. Handing stories down through the generations is not only fascinating, it helps you understand who you are and perhaps why you do the things you do. Respect your elders and listen to them. They do actually know more than you and the benefits of their life experiences are endless.

'Families are like democracies – really rubbish, but better than the alternative.' Unknown

Both my parents were raised in the country, too. All of the men in my family on both sides have been farmers, with the exception of one lawyer, and all the women have been farmers' wives.

Dad's ancestors were among the first and most influential free-settling pastoralists in Australia. Charles and Caroline Armytage bought Como House in South Yarra, Melbourne, in 1864 and the family owned it for over 95 years. Their last surviving children, Constance and Leila, my dad's great aunts, sold it to the National Trust in 1959. We've had many family reunions and happy visits to Como and are proud of this part of our heritage.

My mother was a Flannery. Not surprisingly with a name like Flannery, her heritage is Irish. Her maternal grandmother, Nellie, lost her mother when she was just seven years old in County Cork and when her father remarried she was sent with her sister to live in the care of their uncle, Bishop Gallagher, in Goulburn, New South Wales. Nellie married my great-grandfather, John Vincent Flannery, who was a third-generation farmer on a beautiful property near Boorowa in the central west of New South Wales. Nellie was an academic who loved books and writing, and she missed the rolling green hills of Ireland. She loathed the heat, flies and dust storms.

But although she did not enjoy the rural life, she had a generous heart for those less fortunate. During the Great Depression unemployed men would walk country roads with their swags, looking for work. Known as swaggies, these men were not always well received by farmers, including my great-grandfather.

Nellie put a mark on the mailbox, which was about two kilometres from the house on the main road, to indicate the men were welcome in her home. She would always feed them and give them odd jobs around the property if there were any and then send them on their way.

When my family gets together we are encouraged to perform. None of us can sing or dance but we still hold homemade concerts and recite poetry or sing songs. There's always plenty of chat and laughter around the table, always large, to accommodate all of us. We inherited this from Nellie.

On my mum's side of the family (the Catholics) I have 21 first cousins. On Dad's side (Anglican) I have one cousin. Mmmmmmmmm ...

Call your grandmother

I love both my grandmothers to bits. My generation can learn a lot from this wonderful generation of women. We should listen to them. If you're lucky enough to still have your grandmother around, call her. Listen to her stories about her childhood – chances are she'll love to tell them. Try to learn from her. Use her as a mentor and a confidante. Tell her your stories, too, she'll love being entertained.

If she lives close by, offer to help her. Clean her house, empty her gutters, help with the things she can't quite manage anymore. Make sure she's not lonely, chances are she adores you and misses you. I should be so lucky that I have half the strength and wisdom of both my grandmothers.

During my grandmothers' early married lives, rural properties were extremely isolated. There was no telephone, no vacuum cleaners and certainly no takeaway food. They were not complainers. They suffered in silence but they did not suffer fools. They grew up during the war years, so there was plenty of hardship, but also later there was plenty of glamour.

Rather than compete with other women they encouraged and supported them, without having to crow about it. They were simple cooks, but could throw together a dinner party for twenty at short notice from the pantry and the freezer. They ate good food and walked almost everywhere. Neither of them ever set foot in a gym yet they weren't overweight.

They were self-sacrificing. If shearing was on and the property was busy their lives were on hold and they never complained. As a young girl (when you know everything) I thought this was a sign of weakness and being a pushover. I now realise it shows immense strength and resilience.

They were strong, yet feminine. Nanny Flannery was a city girl who moved with her dashing new airforce pilot husband to a property outside Cowra. It was all foreign to her, but she embraced it and had a go, helping with shearing and mustering, although she discovered she was not a horsewoman. In her early days on the property when she was put on a horse it bolted and she never tried to ride one again. She baked for the week every Monday morning in the Aga stove, cooked lunches for the workmen and raised six children.

Granny Armytage was a tall, elegant woman, full of grace and calm. The Riverina was in her blood and in the early 1940s, when all the men were away at war, she ran the family property near Urana single-handedly, at the age of just twenty. She was a brilliant horsewoman, and could drive a truck or a tractor; she did whatever was needed. She said this was actually one of the happiest times of her life.

When you're isolated in the country, socialising is vital. Granny would take a horse and sulky and drive the 100-mile round trip to Urana (staying overnight) for tennis on the weekends. This was the height of their social diary. Throughout her life tennis was one of her great loves.

My grandfather, Dad's dad, served in the army in New Guinea and was serving in Darwin when it was bombed in 1942 – he never talked about it except to tell us as kids how he and his mates would go fishing on their days off out of Darwin using hand grenades! When Grandpa returned from the war he and Granny were married in South Yarra.

They lived at Dunkeld in Victoria when my father was a young boy – and although Granny missed her home in the Riverina she was content in the country and happy raising their children. She taught my dad to ride as a young boy – he is an excellent horseman now – and was eternally patient. Dad recalls having a friend over to stay when they were aged about five – and the boys decided to go for a swim in a 44 gallon drum of sump oil they stumbled across in one of Grandpa's sheds.

The young boys came to the back door of the house covered in oil up to their necks. Granny didn't bat an eyelid. Dad can't quite remember how Granny scrubbed the oil off but says it was kind of painful. She didn't yell – Dad thinks she probably laughed, but the boys never saw it.

Grandpa was a successful grazier, breaking the world record – a pound for a pound of wool – in 1952. They then moved to Hay in New South Wales in the early '60s and Granny was delighted to be back in the Riverina. Their house in Church Street was the drop-in house for every person who came into town from properties across the district (remember, when you live in the sticks, going '*into town*' is really exciting!). Granny and Grandpa's house was a home away from home for young jackaroos. There was always a warm meal, some great stories and an instant party.

As a little girl – I remember the sound of ice tinkling in glasses and Granny's loud laugh above all the other laughter in Hay. Granny had a huge heart and was very active in the local church, the Red Cross and she started the town's Meals on Wheels service. She was always laughing and sang very loudly in church. Bless.

> *Remember your grandmother won't always be around, so make an effort to see her every time you can. Hug her every time you see her like you may never see her again. Don't ever have any regrets.*

Who can you trust?

Try to be close to your family, they may be the only people you can really trust. They may annoy you and drive you crazy at times, but it's good for your soul to get on with them. It will bring enormous peace to your life.

Everyone has a private side and it should feel comfortable to show this side to your family. When I have a meltdown (never at work, it's unprofessional!), it's important to be able to turn to people you trust for support. No one else on the planet will forgive you your weaknesses like your family, probably because your weaknesses are usually their weaknesses too.

I trust my family's advice 100 per cent, because they don't have an agenda. I don't work for them, I am not contracted to them. They love me unconditionally and they genuinely want the best for me, beyond the end of my next contract.

Of course nobody's family is perfect. Look for the things your family does well and remember only your siblings know exactly what your upbringing was like. When the chips are down they're about the most loyal people you'll find.

Forgive them any wrongs, go easy on them and be there for them in return.

Perhaps I'll leave the last word on family to Gloria from the TV show *Modern Family*: 'Be the wind at their backs, not the spit in their face.' (It sounded better when she said it in Spanish!)

*F*amily is fundamental: in a nutshell

- Be proud of where you've come from.

- Embrace your differences.

- Your parents are doing the best job they can.

- Trust your family and keep them close, their support is vital when the chips are down.

- Be there for your family, too.

- Families genuinely want the best for each other. Treat them with respect.

- Love your siblings, they're the only ones who know what your upbringing was really like.

- Ring your grandmother, help her, hug her and listen to her stories.

- Respect your elders.

Be the leading
lady in the movie
of your life

CHAPTER TEN

*W*hen I was handed the reins at Sunrise in 2013, it was the biggest promotion of my life and it has been the highlight of my career so far. I hadn't coveted the position, but I'd done seven years on the bench at Weekend Sunrise and had worked my butt off for the previous eight years as a news reporter. Plus I'd filled in for what seemed like everyone in the building, so I'd more than earned my place.

But it wasn't all roses. Awful things were written about me. Defamatory things like I wasn't coping; the network had sent me to a health farm to 'recuperate'; that I was being angry in the office; that I was falling out with my colleagues. It was all untrue. I tried to keep it in perspective.

Most of the press I received was fair, but being a typical woman I only listened to the negative stuff. I had been warned I would become interesting to people and I know it's a competitive industry and a *sought-after job, but nothing could have prepared me for this much attention.*

The show's ratings were skyrocketing and the vibe on set had never been better. I picked the brains of my mentors for advice on how to sit still in this storm of publicity and not bite from this poisoned apple, but perhaps the best advice came from my boss.

One day in his office when I was really feeling under pressure, he said to me: 'Are you behaving like the leading lady in the movie of your life right now?' (It pays to remember the TV business is all a giant game.)

'No,' I replied.

'Well start,' he said. 'You're not the second-string best-friend character here, so stop behaving like it.'

I breathed deeply, pulled my shoulders back and went back to being Sam.

There comes a time when the movie of your life ceases to be of the Disney Princess fairytale variety, and it gets real and gritty. In this lifetime, I guarantee not everyone is going to like you. Not everyone is going to respect you. Not everyone is going to listen to you. Not everything is going to go smoothly.

There are going to be women who look better than you in jeans, who are better at your job than you, who seem to form more functional relationships than you, women who seem to have it all. But there will also be plenty of women out there who are threatened by you.

The rise of social media means people can now paint – and literally filter – their lives to be perfect and wonderful, even when the truth is far more grey, and it can all leave you feeling miserable about your lot in life. The trick is attitude. As I've said in these pages, try to make the most of what you've got and avoid comparing yourself to others. While it's human nature, it's a bad habit and it will drive you cray-cray.

Embrace your differences. I used to loathe my body and weight being written about in the papers at the start of my career, until I realised it was what made me different. So I wasn't a stick insect, but I felt great. And women related to me. So I embraced it.

Don't envy others. Attractive, intelligent people can sometimes be miserable (they can also be terribly happy) and even supermodels are airbrushed in magazine photos. As Cindy Crawford once said: 'Even I don't wake up looking like Cindy Crawford.'

Our movie heroine is proactive and her glass is half full. She deals with the tough stuff with panache. She holds her line. She forgives and she isn't bitter about life.

At all costs, try to avoid bitterness.
Not only does it bring you down, it
brings down everyone around you.
Be gentle and kind to yourself and
accept what and who you are.

Improve the things you aren't quite happy with, but play to your differences and choose your life. I often refer to my favourite autobiography, *Open* by Andre Agassi, because from cover to cover I find it so incredibly inspiring. Andre hated tennis, but he knew he had a talent for it and he knew it was his calling. Even though he didn't want to be training or travelling or playing much of the time, he said 'choosing' to do something is so much easier than fighting it.

It's like getting up at 3.40 every morning. If I fought against this, then my life would be a nightmare. Instead, I make a choice to accept it and I jump out of bed every morning and attack the day.

Nobody but you has the right to dictate what you do and what you think in the movie of your life. Whatever your size, shape, colour, religion or sexual orientation, don't be afraid to be yourself. Do whatever makes you happy, as long as it doesn't hurt others. Even if the majority of people around you are bagging you, stick to your guns and deal with it. All the coffee drinkers at *Sunrise* used to tease me about drinking green tea in the mornings because it was better for me, now they all drink it, too.

This is the movie of your life. They're YOUR adventures. YOU are the protagonist, so you have to act like it. Your life is an occasion, rise to it.

Write your own script

- Do you have trouble standing up for yourself?
- Do you take things personally when they weren't really about you?
- Do you ever agree to do things you don't particularly want to do?
- Do you let people walk all over you because you don't stand up to them (then complain about it at home later that night)?
- Do you feel exhausted and rushed all the time?
- Do you sometimes feel like you don't know where you end and others begin?

Of course you do, because you're a woman. This is why you need to write your own script: setting boundaries is one of the most important things you can do to ensure you're not overwhelmed each day and to make sure you retain 'you'. This is essential to healthy relationships both at home and at work, and to ensure one doesn't bleed into the other. It's not fair to take your stress from home and take it out on your workmates or vice versa.

A busy woman's guide to setting boundaries

- Be aware of what you do and don't want
- Know your values
- Have boundaries within yourself – be disciplined!
- Don't feel guilty: people get over it when you say 'no' occasionally
- Communicate and stand your ground politely
- Structure your day: make your gym/yoga/life-coaching sessions as important as your meetings
- Be organised so that you're not working late to make up for what you should have been doing during the day
- Stay strong: don't give in or people won't think you mean it
- Be prepared to cope: know that people *will* test your limits
- Try not to check your phone (emails/Facebook/Instagram/ Twitter) after dinner: let the night be peaceful with the people you love and if you live alone, be peaceful with yourself

Sometimes it feels like my younger sister is my older sister. She's a Leo; enough said. She's incredibly strong-willed and hugely disciplined (she runs marathons!) and she has a background in psychology.

So as Dad says, she likes to analyse us all over Christmas lunch. She's married with two beautiful kids.

At times she's had opinions on my boyfriends, my career and my life. Some I've listened to. Others I've ignored.

We're 23 months apart and I absolutely adore her, she's my best friend, but, like many siblings, sometimes when she's trying to be 'helpful', without knowing it, she can actually be not helpful at all. But, when it comes down to it, I know she's always there for me.

YOU are the priority

Don't be afraid to put yourself first. There's nothing wrong with being selfish when it comes to your own wellness; in fact, it's imperative to your mental and physical health and your quality of life. Practise saying the word 'NO' in the mirror if need be. You don't have to be rude, just firm.

When someone is pestering you or overloading you, be prepared and be patient. Say, 'I'm really sorry that I can't help you with that at the moment as my schedule is overloaded' or, 'Thanks for thinking of me, but I'll have to pass on this one' or, 'Keep me in mind for the future.' People will move on and find someone else to help them. It pays to remember you're not irreplaceable! And people will actually respect you more if you're not a pushover.

I get pretty tired during the week so I decline most social invitations. Politely declining an invitation is perfectly acceptable. Men seem to be much better at doing this than women, so we should take a leaf out of their books.

Losing the plot

In every good movie there is a plot and things get rocky for our heroine. This makes us want her to win even more. People can be mean, relationships sometimes don't work and awful things happen to very good people. Sometimes it makes no sense.

A few years ago my best friend from school, the sweetest, most content and balanced girl in the world and her equally divine husband, lost a baby at 38 weeks. It was horrendous. There was no rhyme or reason. Everything seemed to be going along normally. This was their first baby and our group of friends had held a baby shower for her. We were all deeply shocked. Bad things happen to good people. It pays to be resilient and be able to hold your own hand.

Be kind to yourself and be your own best friend.

At our best and our worst times, it is the people closest to us who really matter. This means making sure you believe in yourself and love yourself so much that you have chosen reliable and trustworthy people around you in all areas of your life. Make sure your friends are doing the right thing by you. Choose to keep friends who are happy for you, not competing with you or finding enjoyment in your misfortune. If they're not doing the right thing by you, reconsider the relationship. Be good to your family, too, because the time will come when you need to lean on them.

Relationships

Now in every good movie the fabulous heroine also needs a love interest. The problem is, while we're all fantastic, or at least working to improve ourselves, some of the men out there leave a lot to be desired. Besides anything else, you have to prove yourself to be more interesting than their smartphone!

> *Be careful who you choose to*
> *marry or share yourself with.*

So it pays to have good judgment. Good judgment comes from experience and experience comes from bad judgment. Yup, I have the t-shirt on this one.

My mother once said to me, 'Sam, you have worse taste in men than Princess Diana.' And that was before she met Dodi! I have dated a man who could not drive a manual car (deal-breaker); a man who wore a thumb ring (also a deal-breaker); and not one, but two men who were unemployed and lived off me. I once went to a seemingly lovely man's house for dinner. He refused to speak, but played the guitar and sang at me all night. Needless to say, I left before dessert. I've also dated a pilot (ugh), a rugby front rower (double ugh, no neck!), a sociopath who, for the sake of this book, I'll downgrade to an extreme narcissist; and too many men who cheated.

Oh, and an abnormal number of men who were *very* close to their mothers.

The best advice I can give you is that any prospective man should be kind, have integrity and inner strength, and preferably have a job – we all need something to do every day! I believe that being kind is the most important. You should also have some central things in common, like your values. Take it from me, a relationship will not work if you have different values. Opposites might attract, but they will find it tough to stay together if they're disagreeing over little/big things like finances, work ethic and where you're going to educate your kids.

If you think you really like a man I also believe you should go on ten, yes TEN, dates with him before you sleep with him. Then you'll know if he's the real deal – and has a job – and you won't give yourself to someone who's not worthy.

When you're dating:

- Don't spend all your time with him – make sure you keep your life going
- Be yourself – I know this is hard in the early stages but it might mean you dodge a bullet in the long term
- Do still play hard to get – there's value in the old-fashioned way and most men do like to do the chasing
- Recognise when he's just not that into you
- Make sure your needs are being met, too
- Treat him well but treat it like a tennis match: you make a move, he makes a move. Avoid calling him incessantly, that's stalking, not dating.

My grandmother once told me to watch a man and how he handles three important things. His reaction to these will tell you everything you need to know about him.

1. A rainy day
2. Tangled Christmas tree lights
3. Lost luggage

Tying the knot

There is no ideal time to get married. You have to do it when you're ready, or perhaps not at all. It's a want, not a need.

I'm so pleased it's completely acceptable to get married later these days. My mother was married at 21. Remember what you were doing at 21? My goodness, I could barely decide what to wear in the mornings, let alone make a decision about who I might spend the rest of my life with. We all mature at a different rate and it's worth taking the time and choosing wisely. If there are any doubts about a bloke, don't marry him. Remember, be a good animal, trust your instincts!

One of my aunts tells the story of walking down the aisle and feeling a niggle in the pit of her stomach, telling her something wasn't right. Sure enough, she has been through a whole lot of pain and is now divorced. I'm so pleased with myself for not having married any of my boyfriends in the past (I've been asked!) because I'd be divorced by now. Ain't nobody got time for that.

I'm also glad I haven't had kids yet because I wouldn't have been the best mother. I feel like I have so much more to give now that my life is on track. I'm calm, I know myself and I love myself. My time will come. There's no pressure; everybody's journey is different.

I feel that when I do get married it should be to someone who is first and foremost a friend. Someone I trust and of course, have the hots for, but making sure it's more than lust. I will no longer be flirting with other men, so I need to be completely sure. I'll ask myself, will I still want to talk to this bloke when we're sitting opposite each other in the nursing home? It pays to remember men have a shorter life expectancy than us, it's the only break we get!

I wouldn't expect marriage to validate you. I don't expect it to be perfect, or easy. It can change you. I'll get married when I'm ready to have a bit of chaos in my life: another person brings a whole new set of worries and dreams that I, like most women, will take on.

I believe that when you realise that you are ready to love rather than just being loved, you are ready for marriage.

When you're in a relationship, it's not all about you.

Needy is a no-no

My name is Samantha Armytage and I confess: in the past, out of neediness, I have dated completely inappropriate men. Neediness makes you stay too long at the party. You know the scenario … when you're 35 and you think you *should* be married so you stay with a completely inappropriate man, even if you're miserable, just to be in a relationship.

If you're feeling needy, you may need to work on your self-esteem. Remember someone else will not permanently make you feel better about yourself. You are the only person who can do that. It's okay for someone else to make you happy, but they shouldn't be your only source of happiness.

Sometimes if you're feeling needy you might have problems trusting your partner. If you don't trust the person you're with, ask yourself why. If it's because they're not trustworthy – they're making shady phone calls, can't tell you where they are, and they're lying to you – get rid of them. That's a deal-breaker. If they're doing the right things the issue is probably yours, so you need to explore this side of yourself. Even if you've been hurt or cheated on before, not every man is like that.

Listen to your instincts. Your tummy will tell you whether or not they're a good person and the situation is right. If you know deep down a person is wrong for you, please face up to that and do something about it sooner rather than later. The less time you spend with a man who's not worthy of you, the less painful it is to leave him. You'll never regret it.

I speak from experience here. I once had a first date in my twenties that was so appalling I put myself in a taxi and left. It was obvious he was not right for me, and I was young enough not to bat an eyelid.

Fast-forward nine years and I ran into him at a party. He asked me out on our 'second first date', laughing at how badly he had behaved the first time round. I was older and needier so I agreed to go. Three months into this relationship I realised I should get out. Then, stupidly, I thought, I'll just get through my birthday. Then it was, I'll just get through Christmas.

I was very uncertain. My family and friends were worried. Then one day I was cleaning out a cupboard … okay, okay, I was snooping. I knew his hiding place! In the pocket of one of his jackets I found a box containing the most enormous diamond ring. It was so huge it would have given me back problems. I instantly felt sick to my stomach.

If this is how the thought of a marriage proposal makes you feel, it's a deal-breaker. All of a sudden, I realised I'd wasted a year of my life on a man who didn't deserve me.

I stood strong and made a decision. This is the one I am most proud of in my life: I decided that I was better off by myself and as Bridget Jones would say, 'found half-eaten by Alsatians', alone in my own apartment, than married, and no doubt subsequently divorced from that man.

All the single ladies

Ask yourself, why do I do what I do, when I know what I know? The answer is, because neediness takes over. That's okay, be gentle on yourself. You'll work it out.

Some people find it safer to be in a relationship and they're tired of being lonely. Take it from me, the wrong relationship is the loneliest place in the world. YOU WILL BE OKAY ON YOUR OWN. I promise you.

Being on your own and doing fun things, healthy things, nurturing things, is so much better than hanging around wasting precious time with a jerk.

Remember:

- Being single is fun and gives you freedom
- Having a relationship is a want, not a need
- Being independent and secure in yourself will actually make you more attractive to a potential mate
- Value yourself!

I used to liken myself to a car with the airconditioner on when I was in a relationship. I could still go, but I wasn't really moving through my life at full power. That's when it hit me that I was attracting the wrong types, and then staying in the wrong relationships. The right relationship shouldn't make you feel like you're being held back.

If you really want to meet someone, you will. You will never be a great partner for someone until you're being great to yourself. Take it from me.

*B*e the leading lady in the movie of your life: in a nutshell

- Not everyone is going to like you.

- Don't compare yourself with others, we're all different.

- Understand and try to avoid negative emotions such as envy and bitterness.

- Be yourself and choose the starring role you want to take in your life.

- Write your own script: set boundaries and teach people how to treat you.

- YOU are the priority.

- Be your own best friend.

- Be careful who you trust.

- Pick a man who's kind.

- Be a good animal, trust your instincts.

- Avoid neediness.

- Never date a man who doesn't deserve you.

- Marriage isn't the be-all and end-all of life.

- Being single is fun!

Afterword

I mostly exist in a very 'yang' world. There's a lot of masculine energy in the television industry. And I don't just mean the men.

It's an aggressive, cynical world where the news cycle revolves around fierce deadlines, breaking news, immediacy, progress and pushing forward.

Then when I leave work, I race around town, stuck in traffic, doing chores, on my phone.

My challenge – and the challenge for lots of women nowadays – is balance.

To make it more 'yin'. Quieten it down, be present and embrace my feminine.

I consider myself to be a girl's girl anyway, but daily I have to remind myself of that and get back to me.

Luckily my job at *Sunrise* includes lots of lovely, positive, uplifting experiences.

We often get to make a difference and help those in need – and an added bonus is that I work with some brilliant, generous women AND some fantastic, talented men.

After a few experiences with unhappy, vindictive women, it was getting easier to think 'women are their own worst enemy' and 'all women are dreadful'.

But I didn't want to let myself go down that path. I choose to look for the good, to pay attention to all the wonderful, supportive, clever, sometimes vulnerable, not-always-perfect-but-doing-their-best women in my life:

- In my family
- At work
- From school
- From university
- In the street.

They're there – you just have to recognise and nurture them.

Modern feminism isn't about blaming men for our faults or the things that don't work out for us – we take responsibility for ourselves.

- We need to encourage other women, not judge them
- We need to support each other and, most importantly, we need to back ourselves
- We also need to encourage, admire and love our men and try not to compete with them
- We must make the most of ourselves each day.

So I've written this book – and ticked it off my bucket list, yay! – as a kind of therapy for myself, but also for you guys.

I'd love to know what you think of it.

Please let me know – and share your stories and experiences with me using the hashtag *#Shine* and we can get this conversation started.

Go get 'em, girls ...

Thank you!

With special thanks to: my publisher, Robert Watkins, for being so encouraging and patient (and laughing at all my jokes).

Mum and Dad for lending me their verandah to get some peace and quiet to write, and Jake the labrador for sitting by my feet and keeping me company.

My sister, Georgie, for being my bestie.

All the guys at *Sunrise* for being so understanding over the past year while I was writing/shooting two shows/getting up at 3.30am!

All the gals at boarding school who didn't realise they were giving me so much fodder for the future.

And all the wonderful, strong, supportive, fabulous, hilarious, generous, kind, fun women in my life who just make things a little bit better.

X

I'm proud to be an ambassador for Soldier On. It's an organisation set up to help support our physically and psychologically wounded servicemen and women – and their families.

Soldier On aims to help in their rehabilitation as well as inspire and empower them.

Australia punches far above its weight on battlefields around the world. But war is only part of it. Sometimes when they get home, another battle begins. Post-traumatic stress disorder affects too many of our returned soldiers and in turn, their families.

I hope this book can put a smile on the faces of our returned servicewomen and the wonderful wives, girlfriends, mothers, sisters and daughters of the men who go off to defend our country.

PROUDLY SUPPORTING

Samantha Armytage is an ambassador
for the Australian charity Soldier On.
www.soldieron.org.au

Find Sam on Twitter

@sam_armytage

Instagram

@sam_armytage

Share your stories and experiences with Sam using the hashtag

#Shine